COVERING CONGRESS

Media Studies Series

America's Schools and the Mass Media,
edited by Everette E. Dennis and Craig L. LaMay

Children and the Media,
edited by Everette E. Dennis and Edward C. Pease

Covering Congress,
edited by Everette E. Dennis and Robert W. Snyder

The Culture of Crime,
edited by Everette E. Dennis and Craig L. LaMay

Defining Moments in Journalism,
edited by Nancy J. Woodhull and Robert W. Snyder

Higher Education in the Information Age,
edited by Everette E. Dennis and Craig L. LaMay

Journalists in Peril,
edited by Nancy J. Woodhull and Robert W. Snyder

The Media in Black and White,
edited by Everette E. Dennis and Edward C. Pease

Media and Democracy,
edited by Everette E. Dennis and Robert W. Snyder

Media Mergers,
edited by Nancy J. Woodhull and Robert W. Snyder

Media and Public Life,
edited by Everette E. Dennis and Edward C. Pease

Publishing Books,
edited by Everette E. Dennis, Craig L. LaMay, and Edward C. Pease

Radio—The Forgotten Medium,
edited by Edward C. Pease and Everette E. Dennis

COVERING CONGRESS

edited by
Everette E. Dennis
Robert W. Snyder

Transaction Publishers
New Brunswick (U.S.A.) and London (U.K.)

Copyright © 1998 by Transaction Publishers, New Brunswick, New Jersey 08903. Originally published in the *Media Studies Journal,* Winter 1996. Copyright © 1996 by The Freedom Forum Media Studies Center and The Freedom Forum.

All rights reserved under International and Pan-American Copyright Conventions. No part of this book may be reproduced or transmitted in any form or by any means, electronic or mechanical, including photocopy, recording, or any information storage and retrieval system, without prior permission in writing from the publisher. All inquiries should be addressed to Transaction Publishers, Rutgers—The State University, New Brunswick, New Jersey 08903.

This book is printed on acid-free paper that meets the American National Standard for Permanence of Paper for Printed Library Materials.

Library of Congress Catalog Number: 97-5091
ISBN: 1-56000-946-2
Printed in the United States of America

Library of Congress Cataloging-in-Publication Data

Covering Congress / edited by Everette E. Dennis and Robert W. Snyder.
    p. cm.
"Originally published in the Media studies journal, Winter 1996"—Verso of t.p.
Includes bibliographical references and index.
ISBN 1-56000-946-2 (pbk. : alk. paper)
    1. Government and the press—United States. 2. United States—Congress—Reporters and reporting. I. Dennis, Everette E. II. Snyder, Robert W., 1955– . III. Media studies journal.
PN4738.C68 1997
070.4'49324'0973—dc21   97-5091
                                                                             CIP

Contents

Preface   xi

Introduction   xv

Part I: Overviews

Congressional Index   3
Carrie Klein

In the congressional press corps there are 71 journalists for every senator and 16 for every representative. Before you conclude that this makes for media savvy on Capitol Hill, consider some of the statistics in this index compiled by a former Senate aide.

1. Congress—Boom Box and Black Box   7
   Ross K. Baker

"There is no better example of Beltway insiderism than the manner in which the legislative process is infused with needless complexity by politicians and shunned or sloppily reported by many journalists," argues a political scientist who has long studied Congress. "The combined effect of the two is to hoodwink the people by a priestly class speaking a language as incomprehensible to ordinary citizens as Ge'ez, the liturgical tongue of the Ethiopian church."

Part II: Media on the Hill

2. Evolution and Revolution   19
   Timothy E. Cook

Newt Gingrich has forged a revolution in the relationship between his office and the media at his own peril, writes a political scientist. "Eventually Gingrich may face a dilemma: having mobilized the media to focus attention on his agenda, he must reckon with the prospect that someday they might pay attention to him at a time when he finds their coverage less useful, if not counterproductive."

3. Getting Out the Message 27
Newt Gingrich

The outspoken speaker of the House offers some highly critical views of the American media, arguing that "they do not cover progress as well as decay. They pander cynically to the basest tastes and look upon any declarations of belief in God or the unique American as corny and unsophisticated."

4. Speed Over Substance 29
Ann Compton

"The broadcasting technology that blanketed Capitol Hill in miles of fiber-optic cable has helped to transform work for the men and women who report on Congress," a veteran Washington reporter notes. "Caught in the daily competition among correspondents, many do not even seem aware of the changes that are certainly shaping the news we report in ways that privilege speed over substance."

5. Getting on the Radar Screen 33
Rachel B. Gorlin

"I know you think that a lot of reporters are jerks, or worse," writes a former congressional press secretary in a satirical memo on the congressional press corps. "In addition, as you've heard me say before, journalists are like dogs—they sense when you don't like them or are afraid of them, which is when they move in for the kill."

6. Toward Civic-minded Media 43
Bill Bradley

As he prepared to leave his seat, the New Jersey senator commented on the media's contribution to negativity in politics. "I am saddened on occasion when the media, and politicians themselves, convey that politics is mean, cheap and dirty; that what we hold in common as Americans is somehow less than what we harbor in our hearts and minds for ourselves as individuals. I have never believed that."

7. Making News, Making Law 45
    Ronald D. Elving

"The family-leave story offers an unusually vivid case study of how media attitudes toward a bill can change over time and of how those attitudes may affect a bill's fate," according to a congressional journalist. "It is also useful in demonstrating how the media may miss, or at least fail to communicate, much of what is really going on when a bill becomes a law."

8. Behind the Noise on the Floor 55
    Donald Rothberg

"We have to try to get away from the stock stories that might have run years ago, in which it was basically, 'Senator so-and-so said this...,'" writes a veteran Washington reporter for the Associated Press. "The AP and other press institutions have made the decision that what's really important is what is behind the noise that's coming from the floor."

9. Big Picture and Local Angle 57
    Melissa Merson

The meeting of high-speed communications technology and congressional tradition is producing unique journalistic hybrids, asserts a Washington legislative analyst. "If the news from Congress keeps coming faster and faster, how will anyone find the time to think about what it all means?"

10. New Media, Old Messages 65
    Graeme Browning

"Despite the evidence that literally millions of Americans confer regularly through the Internet and despite lightning-like advances in technology, most members of Congress don't seem to have a clue about how to employ the Net to advantage," writes a Washington reporter. "Except in a handful of instances, politicians in Washington are using the new technology to convey an old message."

Part III: Beyond the Beltway

11. Getting the Whole Truth   75
    Brian Lamb

C-SPAN's chairman and CEO reiterates that "our most important task, by far, remains our original one—daily gavel-to-gavel coverage of congressional floor debates. Ironically, however, Congress has actually restricted citizens' ability to watch its deliberations on television in two ways: by limiting what the cameras installed in the Capitol can show and by enacting legislation that has caused cutbacks in the distribution of C-SPAN telecasts of the House and Senate."

12. Showtime for Democracy   81
    Reuven Frank

Members of Congress, writes the former president of NBC News, have long chafed under the president's ability to command the attention of the media. "If their vital constitutional task of legislating could not win the attention of the folks back home, there was one stage on which members of Congress, too, could play with their exits and their entrances and their many parts—congressional oversight hearings."

13. Hollywood Goes to Congress   89
    Tom Rosenstiel

Films on Congress flatter no one, observes a former congressional reporter. And over the years the image of congressional journalists has gone from "bad (smart but jaded opportunists) to better (earnest but jaded opportunists) to bland (powerful and manipulable opportunists)."

14. Coverage—The Void at Home   99
    Martin Weinberger

"The void in newspaper coverage of Congress creates an opportunity for the attentive legislator," writes the publisher and editor in chief of a California newspaper. "Through press releases, video material, district pork, local office contacts, subsidized mailings, awards and honors to residents, capital visits by constituents and use of staff, members of Congress can use newspapers to color the quality and depth of their work and to help fend off any challenges to re-election."

15. Kingmakers, Kingbreakers 105
Shirley Williams

"The tone of American congressional coverage is what one might call superior skepticism," a British politician, professor and member of the House of Lords observes. "The skepticism is the product of congressional self-laceration. The superior note comes from the media's self-perception as watchdog, scourge and purifier."

Part IV: Media and Congress in Historical Perspective

16. Not a Pretty Picture 113
Joan L. Conners

"People looking for positive portrayals of Congress will not find them in political cartoons," writes a doctoral candidate who has compiled a portfolio of congressional images. "Since the 18th century, cartoons have expressed skepticism about the contributions of Congress to American political life and the character of congressional leaders."

17. Unexpected Consequences—New Media and Congress 125
Thomas C. Leonard

"When Congress cheers on a communications revolution, what does it get for its money and its high hopes?" asks a historian of journalism. "Throughout history, advances in reporting have turned our political order sour at least as often as they have brought sweetness and light."

18. Race, Rules and Reporting 131
Donald A. Ritchie

"The mainstream press in Washington long operated under rules that effectively barred minority journalists," says a historian of congressional reporting. "Integration of the Washington press corps was a slow and painful process, complicated by white reporters' intolerance and indifference, discord within the African American press and rancor between men and women journalists of both races."

19. Rayburn, the Workhorse 139
Joe S. Foote

From the 1940s until the 1960s, Speaker of the House Sam Rayburn wielded enormous power without courting the national media. "In retrospect," notes a media scholar and former congressional press secretary, "Rayburn's methods for dealing with the press provide a benchmark for measuring the evolution of congressional influence upon the media and media influence on Congress."

Part V: Books

20. Many Questions, Few Answers 149
Jeffrey R. Biggs

"Are Congress and the media simply caught in a series of combative encounters that must inexorably repeat themselves without abatement?" asks a former press secretary to a speaker of the House. "Scholarship has yet to offer definitive answers to such questions, but it has provided some perspective to clarify where our concerns should really lie."

For Further Reading 161

Index 163

Preface

News media in the United States and the Congress of the United States have more in common than they readily admit. Both are commonly regarded as institutions of society by scholars and commentators and both purport to "represent" the people. The Congress, of course, has that duty officially by law. The news media makes this claim more symbolically.

Perhaps for this reason more than any other the bare-knuckled conflicts and multiple misunderstandings separating media and government are seen most vividly in the coverage (and sometimes noncoverage) of Congress by the print and electronic media.

For an institution that likes to think of itself as the "necessary representative" of the people, the press has been less than dynamic in its surveillance of the Congress as compared with the executive branch or presidency. Congress, whose 535 members (in the House and Senate combined) are part of a complex and often glacial process, is often hard to track and difficult to assess. Congress is a responsive institution and only rarely initiates. While each piece of legislation has a beginning and an endpoint, the distance between the two often bores those who are driven by immediacy and by defining moments or great decisions.

Through much of the nineteenth century and the early years of the twentieth, the national legislature was more powerful than the executive, but still had an identity dispersed over hundreds of people, thousands of bills and scores of committees. The focal point was rarely clear, so even in times of weak presidents, the executive still had more public attention.

In 1994, a new Republican majority led by Speaker Newt Gingrich came to power and promised to change the stakes for Congress vis-à-vis the other branches of government. At times it appeared that the new speaker, who led what he called a Republican revolution promoting a "Contract with America," did get more coverage than Congress had at any previous time in the twentieth century. Over the next two years, coverage of Congress continued at a heightened and steady pace, though it did not outdistance coverage of the presidency of Bill Clinton. Its relative visibility, however, accelerated and even when the speaker was punished for ethics violations in January 1997, Congress continued to be in the eye of a storm, one that the news media watched with intense interest and covered extensively.

That trend, which continues as this is written, bodes well for better and more coherent presentation of this representative institution to readers and viewers everywhere. The Congress as a visible expression of the electorate is a dynamic process whose will and ways must be understood for anyone to truly know what government is doing and why. For this reason, more rigorous coverage of an institution sometimes neglected by the press is imperative.

This book began as an issue of the *Media Studies Journal* under my stewardship and that of managing editor Robert Snyder in late 1994 and early 1995. It is transformed here into a book because of repeated requests. Used as a text in college and university courses, the *Journal* issue published in winter 1996 won critical acclaim and quickly exhausted its warehouse stock. With some modifications, we are pleased to introduce this work anew with the hope that it will lead both to better public understanding of Congress and better media coverage of this great institution.

While both the Congress and the press claim the mandate of representation, that is, "re-presenting" the views of the public in the context of public policy and public understanding, their mutual cooperation in connecting more directly in the realm of public communication benefits everyone. In this volume, with the help of expert authors, we explain why the two institutions are sometimes at loggerheads, with the press seeking information and the Congress sometimes finding that unruly process difficult if not maddening.

There is no legal requirement that the two work together, indeed, it might now even by claimed that cyberspace permits the legislative bodies to bypass the mainstream press. This, however, would be a great mistake, since the press with all of its frailties and deficiencies does more than foster the free flow of information. Instead the media offer descriptive detail, background and interpretation as well as methods of assessing outcomes and speculating about the future. This is truly value-added in an age of truncated information and sensationalization.

A cooperative connection between the Congress and the media stands to benefit both. For the Congress, this facilitates access to millions of citizens and voters; for the media it means easier access to information and the stuff from which news is formulated and dispensed.

In the pages that follow, historians and political scientists join journalists and commentators, critics and analysts in assessing the temperature of congressional-press relations as well as suggesting how this process of public communication might be improved for the benefit of both parties, the public and, we hope, democracy itself.

> Everette E. Dennis
> Senior Vice President
> and Executive Director,
> International Consortium of Universities
> The Freedom Forum

Introduction

Although observers of media-government relations most often think first of conflicts with the executive branch, intersections between Congress and the media have been extensive and varied since the first Washington "correspondents" began sending dispatches from the first sessions of Congress. (One day after it approved the First Amendment, the House considered barring reporters from the floor of the House on the grounds that they cast over their proceedings "a thick veil of misrepresentation and error.")

In recent years the connection between Congress and the news media has grown more complex. Coverage of Congress by the print and electronic media is ever present. At the same time, Congress has increasing power to make communication policy that has important impact on the ability of the media to conduct their affairs, both economically and politically. While recognizing the importance of the latter, this book is dedicated to an exploration of those aspects of the relationship between the media and Congress that shape the news that reaches the information-seeking public.

Until recently, coverage of the Congress most often took a backseat to coverage of the presidency, and for good reason. The presidency is centered around a single individual. Its goals are stated up front, often in bold terms. The Congress, conversely, is all about process— the movement of legislation through a tortured and measured process to the end point of an act that goes to the executive.

What has been largely a quiescent, convoluted branch of government with multiple agendas and impasses with the presidency and sometimes the courts—all of which add up to gridlock—got a rocket boost of energy in 1994. In that year the leadership changed hands, moving from decades of Democratic Party dominance to a Republican ascendancy under Speaker Newt Gingrich. In a January 1985 article, the *Washington Post* wondered whether Gingrich was "just about the most disliked member of Congress." In 1995, *Time* named him "Man of the

Year." The new speaker has been at the center of attention, either in discussions of the election itself, which has been called the Republican "revolution," or in debates over the "Contract with America," a legislative package that he championed, which became a rallying point for the Republican-led Congress.

Gingrich, a more visible public official than almost any of his predecessors, has used the media with telling effect, made himself a lightning rod for criticism and press scrutiny, and generated an avalanche of publicity for both his office and the Congress. Speaker Gingrich has mastered the process of publicity through both the traditional media and through C-SPAN, the cable service covering Congress, where he honed his skills for over a decade. He has also made a considerable reputation for himself as an advocate for communication in cyberspace.

Media coverage of Congress has its origins in official transcripts of congressional debate and the work of "correspondents" who, according to F.B. Marbut's classic study *News from the Capital* (1971), were mostly merchants and politicians who sent letters to the press. Washington reportage came later and evolved over the years. It was sometimes lively and robust, especially during periods when the power of Congress truly challenged the president. But most often the media and Congress were said to be "partners in propaganda," with reporters rewriting news releases. Media scholar Stephen Hess and other commentators have pointed out that members of Congress are rarely national newsmakers. The vast majority of legislators work with and through local media, where their lament is often said to be, "Doesn't anybody know my name?"

While most media executives would say that coverage of Congress is a serious proposition, they rarely reinforce this with sustained and searching attention. While it is usually a sign of quality journalism for a local or regional newspaper to have a Washington correspondent largely concerned with Congress and its connection to their home turf, there is some doubt that this results in enough critical or insightful coverage. If anything, many regional correspondents celebrate "pork." They duly note what Congress is doing for their district and either lionize local members of Congress—exaggerating their role on the national scene—or scrutinize them and their personal lives mercilessly and often without context.

The national media are committed to systematic congressional coverage, although the stars of what Howard Kurtz has called the "media circus" are rarely stationed on Capitol Hill. The White House is still the most prestigious post for a Washington correspondent. Networks, both broadcast and cable, have a strong presence on the Hill, as do national magazines and newspapers. Increasingly, due to new technologies, local and regional television also cover the Hill, but in somewhat sporadic fashion. There are hundreds of specialized newsletters and other media as well as a band of stalwarts who painstakingly make the Congress the focal point of their coverage, including *Congressional Quarterly, National Journal, Roll Call, The Hill* and more.

Congress depends on the media to reach the public but also has considerable muscle to shape its media relations if it has strong leadership and a coherent plan, which it usually lacks. Nevertheless, Congress does much to try to project a friendly face to the public through the media, facilitating interviews in Capitol Hill radio and television studios. Congress also allows television coverage of its proceedings through electronic channels, most notably C-SPAN. Over the years major congressional hearings have become publicity ventures, wherein a committee presents a compelling cast of witnesses and hopes for massive coverage of both their testimony and publicity-seeking committee members.

There are probably almost as many congressional views of the media as there are members of Congress, but in general members often see reporters as enemies, as an adversarial pack armed with embarrassing and sometimes unfair questions that will come between them and their constituents. At the same time, the most successful and well-known members of Congress are usually masters of media relations. Congress can facilitate or obstruct the media, and it often does both.

This book, which is coordinated with The Freedom Forum's "Congress and the Media" project, is presented at a time when Congress is particularly active, when it has a powerful and controversial speaker and when the Senate is replete with presidential candidates seeking attention. Whether the changes set in motion by the 1994 congressional elections signify lasting institutional shifts or merely ephemeral tremors is not yet clear. What is clear, however, is that Congress has connected with the modern communications age and that the consequences of this encounter are likely to be accentuated in the years ahead.

Congress, as one of our contributors notes, is the source of much news and much self-promotion. Yet there is in the United States neither a broad nor deep understanding of our national legislature. For journalists, political analysts, citizens and people in government—in short, for all who care about public life—this is a shortcoming that needs to be remedied. The chapters assembled here take up a portion of this task by looking at the overall picture, the media scene on Capitol Hill, the messages that reach beyond the Beltway and the history of relations between the Congress and the press.

Our "Overviews" are provided by Ross K. Baker and Carrie Klein. "Media on the Hill" features essays by Timothy E. Cook, Ann Compton, Rachel B. Gorlin, Ronald D. Elving, Donald Rothberg, Melissa Merson and Graeme Browning, and quotes from House Speaker Newt Gingrich, R-Ga., and Sen. Bill Bradley, D-N.J. "Beyond the Beltway" includes articles by Brian Lamb, Reuven Frank, Tom Rosenstiel, Martin Weinberger and Shirley Williams. "Media and Congress in Historical Perspective" opens with a portfolio of cartoons compiled by Joan L. Conners, followed by contributions from Thomas C. Leonard, Donald A. Ritchie and Joe S. Foote. Our review essay is by Jeffrey R. Biggs.

Everette E. Dennis
Robert W. Snyder

Part I
Overviews

Congressional Index

Carrie Klein

Number of journalists accredited to the U.S. Senate and U.S. House of Representatives press galleries: 7142[1]
Number of U.S. senators: 100
Ratio of journalists to senators: 71:1
Number of U.S. representatives: 435
Ratio of journalists to U.S. representatives: 16:1

Number of U.S. senators and representatives who worked as attorneys before entering Congress: 204[2]
Number who worked as journalists: 24[3]
Ratio of attorneys to journalists in Congress: 8.5:1

Year human features first transmitted by television: 1925[4]
Year U.S. House of Representatives first allowed television cameras to broadcast its proceedings: 1979[5]
Year U.S. Senate first allowed television cameras to broadcast its proceedings: 1986[6]

Percentage of U.S. representatives who have been elected since the House proceedings were first televised: 83[7]
Percentage who have been elected since the Macintosh personal computer was introduced: 65[8]
Percentage who have e-mail addresses: 30[9]

Average age of a U.S. senator: 59
Average age of a U.S. senator with both e-mail and a home page on the Internet: 56
Average age of a U.S. senator with neither e-mail nor a home page on the Internet: 63[10]

Number of U.S. Senate receptionists who did not know what a home page on the Internet was: 21

Number of U.S. senators with home pages on the Internet whose receptionist did not know what a home page was: 6[11]

Number of telephone access lines per square mile in Wyoming: 2.63
Number of telephone access lines per square mile in the District of Columbia: 12,545[12]

Number of Americans who watch C-SPAN at least once during an average week: 16.7 million[13]
Number who watch at least one National Football League game during an average week in football season: 80 million[14]

Number of Americans who watched C-SPAN at least once during a recent 12-month period: 68 million[15]
Number who watched the O.J. Simpson "Bronco chase": 95 million[16]
Number who watched the O.J. Simpson verdict: 150 million[17]

Percentage of Americans 18 and over who watch television: 92[18]
Percentage who listen to the radio: 85[19]
Percentage who read a newspaper: 83[20]
Percentage who voted in the 1992 presidential election: 55[21]
Percentage who voted in the 1994 congressional elections: 39[22]

1. Source: Merrie Baker, U.S. Senate press gallery, Washington.
2. Michael Barone and Grant Ujifusa, *The Almanac of American Politics* 1996 (Washington: National Journal, 1995). There were 533 U.S. senators and representatives when the survey was conducted in November 1995 because of the resignations of U.S. Sen. Robert Packwood, R-Ore., and U.S. Rep. Mel Reynolds, D-Ill.
3. Ibid.
4. *The 1994 Information Please Almanac: The Ultimate Browser's Reference* (Boston: Houghton Mifflin, 1993), p. 112.
5. *Congressional Quarterly's Guide to Congress,* 4th edition (Washington: Congressional Quarterly, 1991) p. 522.
6. Ibid.
7. Barone and Ujifusa, *The Almanac of American Politics* 1996.
8. *The 1994 Information Please Almanac: The Ultimate Browser's Reference.*

9. Survey of the U.S. House of Representatives Constituent Electronic Mail System" on the Thomas system.
10. Telephone survey of 99 Senate offices by Carrie Klein, Nov. 16, 1995. Age information from Barone and Ujifusa, The Almanac of American Politics 1996.
11. Telephone survey of 99 Senate offices by Carrie Klein, Nov. 16, 1995.
12. Source: Amy Fabian, Public Affairs Office, U.S. Telephone Association, Washington.
13. "Unplugged," *National Journal,* Nov. 4, 1995, p. 2735, citing a Mediamark Research study of C-SPAN viewers of voting age.
14. Source: Andrew Fink, Public Relations Department, National Football League, New York.
15. "Unplugged," *National Journal,* Nov. 4, 1995, p. 2736, citing a Statistical Research Inc. study of C-SPAN viewers.
16. "White v. Black," *Newsweek,* Oct. 16, 1995, p. 30.
17. Ibid, p. 31.
18. *Statistical Abstract of the United States,* 1995. Fig. No. 898. "Multimedia Audiences—Summary: 1994," p. 571.
19. Ibid.
20. Ibid.
21. Statistical Abstract of the United States, 1995. Fig. No. 462, "Resident Population of Voting Age and Percent Casting Vote: 1988–1994," p 291.
22. Source: Curtis Gans, Committee for the Study of the American Electorate, Washington.

Carrie Klein was an aide to former Senator Mark O. Hatfield, R-Ore.

1

Congress—Boom Box and Black Box

Ross K. Baker

The process by which public policy is made in the United States is now largely incomprehensible to its citizens. At the heart of public policy-making is Congress, whose members pour forth millions of reams of paper and billions of decibels of sound bites to communicate with bewildered citizens without really improving their understanding of legislative processes. Indeed, much of what flows from Congress advertises rather than teaches, propagandizes rather than enlightens and obfuscates rather than clarifies. Viewed from the outside, Congress is simultaneously a black box, in which invisible wheels, cogs, gears and semiconductors whir away unseen and uncomprehended by Americans, and a loud and vulgar boom box, spewing forth self-serving and fatuous hype, designed to convince people that they are being served by tribunes of unsurpassed virtue and wisdom. The acoustical boost for the politicians' message is provided mostly by journalists. What is less clear is how good a job journalists are doing helping citizens understand the inner workings of Congress. Journalists may be better as amplifiers than as clarifiers.

Messages do flow the other way in the form of letters, phone calls, e-mail and faxes from individuals and interest groups protesting, demanding relief or just venting, but there is no decent exchange between the blaring self-promotion of the officeholders and the entreaties and importunings of the constituents. The messages fly back and forth like so many salvos of arrows loosed by hostile tribes, some of which hit their target while others bury themselves ineffectually in the ground. From the point of view of the members of Congress, knowing what it is that is eating at their constituents is obviously essential in a representative republic, but that is now reduced to a process of divination in which the role of soothsayer is performed by pollsters. And the job does get done well enough for the officeholders to get some sense of the appetites and aversions of their voters. The voters, however, are largely in the dark about how they are governed. It is no simple matter to ascribe causes to this disconnection, to assign responsibility or even to say for certain what the effects are of a governmental process that is significantly less fathomable to citizens than the workings of a VCR. There is a pressing need for a decent, user-friendly owner's manual to government that politicians, for reasons we shall explore in this essay, have little incentive to provide. Journalists are uniquely positioned to provide the technical data to citizens, but it often comes off looking like Fortran.

I want to start first with the causes of citizen incomprehension. I suspect that, to a greater or lesser extent, this has always been a problem. I have reason to believe that the first time the fanciful schematic "How a Bill Becomes Law" was being printed in a civics textbook, bills were becoming laws in a manner quite a bit different from the winged measure shown flying from one house of Congress to the other and then on to the White House. But mostly, there was a legislative process with a beginning and an end that could be explained to citizens, either by a patient politician or journalist, or acquired by citizens themselves willing to incur the modest information costs involved.

Ideally, the legislative process should begin with a member of Congress laying the groundwork for a change in policy by staging an agenda-setting activity, introducing the bill and getting the chairman of a committee to hold hearings. A few interest groups would weigh in for or against, the initiator would lose a few times, reintroduce it and, somewhere down the road, a signing ceremony would take place on the White House lawn, and the member would go back to his office with a framed copy of the measure and some souvenir ballpoint pens.

Yet the process, so far as the most important legislation affecting the largest number of Americans in the most profound ways is concerned, has now become so distended in dimension and problematical in outcome that any effort to diagram it would result in a schematic approximating in complexity the wiring on a nuclear submarine.

Getting on the national agenda may now actually be easier due to the proliferation of media that can cultivate an idea and bring it to the attention of the public. The idea, however, now has greater competition for the attention of the public because there are so many politicians out there using so many media to float so many messages. Journalists can play an important role in winnowing the multitude of claims for places on the national agenda that come from congressional offices, but sadly, they do not usually do a very good job of filtering agenda items in terms of their intrinsic importance. This is not a censorship role: it is, however, one of signaling priorities.

Once policy change takes the form of legislation, it is likely to have to face not one congressional committee but two or perhaps three. This comes about as a result of the practice of multiple referrals, which was designed to spread the action on legislation by giving more than one committee legislative jurisdiction over a bill, and it means more than simply two or three sets of hearings. It means that the interest groups that hover in the gravitational field of each of these committees get involved, and the number of points at which a bill can be altered, or killed altogether, increases.

The coverage of legislative hearings by journalists, however, varies in thoroughness not according to the importance of the legislation under examination, but rather to the celebrity value of the witnesses or their capacity to evoke anger or pathos. If the legislation is at all important, the White House will have become involved, and all kinds of messages will be coursing back and forth along Pennsylvania Avenue. There may be a bill-signing somewhere down the road, but it will be the product of a process that will have involved arcane legislative rules, votes structured in such a way as to allow members to avoid political exposure and considerable public posturing usually characterized by dire threats that typically mask some groping for compromise that is going on behind the scenes. And the result is designed to achieve a Lewis Carroll conclusion: all have won and all shall have prizes.

Admittedly, the process was designed to make change difficult; the framers of the Constitution did not prize legislative efficiency. But neither did they want a system of such baffling opacity that no one could figure out what was going on in government.

In theory, we now have a process that gives programs legal authority to operate and sets a ceiling on the money that they can spend. That is supposed to be followed by a process in which the actual funds are appropriated, and since 1975 there has been a third process by which

Congress harmonizes revenues with expenditures in a reconciliation bill. Yet it is difficult to remember any recent time when the process unfolded with such directness and simplicity. You now have appropriations approved before authorizations, wholesale legislating on appropriations in clear violation of congressional rules and even, in 1982, the sly wink at the constitutional requirement that all revenue bills originate in the House when the Senate initiated that year's Tax Equity and Fiscal Relief Act. And these devices are simple compared to the array of gimmicks—usually associated with fiscal politics—such as lockboxes, fire walls, king-of-the-hill amendments and other procedural legerdemain that render lawmaking as baffling to Americans as the ancient Chinese practice of foot binding.

All resorts to procedural complexity and specialization of vocabulary are a conspiracy against the laity. The laity, in this case, is not only the average citizen with a limited tolerance for insider politics, but also what has been called "the attentive public," a group one step below journalists in political sophistication. Procedural complexity furnishes that rarest and most treasured of all public-sector commodities: political cover. With clarity, however, comes an ability to trace lines of accountability.

The eternal quest for political cover involves the frequent resort to what is euphemistically called "omnibus legislation," a horse-and-rabbit stew that veto proofs some measures that the president despises by embedding them in essential legislation, such as the budget, and also causes the legislation to be so complex that holding members to account for any single part of it becomes almost impossible. Reporters who fail to call attention to the cover mechanisms used by members of Congress to smudge the fingerprints of accountability are, in a real sense, accomplices.

How does this thimble-rigging affect the well-being of American democracy? In a recent essay, the distinguished political scientist Robert Dahl wrote: "If...the workings of the political system have become inscrutable, should we be surprised if a great many voters feel they are powerless to determine what goes on in their government? Can we reasonably expect ordinary citizens to be sufficiently familiar with the 'wiring diagram' of Congress to appraise sensibly how well the institution is working?" Dahl continues by observing that "because the way government works is largely incomprehensible to ordinary citizens, when they look for remedies for what they see as the defects of government their diagnoses are likely to be inappropriate."

If the procedures adopted by lawmakers in a representative republic confuse its citizens, this does not lead, in my mind, to an argument for direct democracy or government by plebiscite. Rather it imposes on elected officials an obligation to fashion more understandable procedures. It also imposes on journalists an obligation to present these procedures in a manner that can aid in that understanding.

The cause of clarity is not always abetted by the media. Many years ago, the respected journalist Edward G. Lowry observed, "One of the reasons why a generally false impression of Congress is diffused throughout the country is the practice of newspapers of printing only the interesting things that happen on the floor of the two chambers...[so] that when the public outside of Washington reads of the House of Representatives, it is always in connection with some scene that is dramatic or important or picturesque."

Journalists quite rightly detest covering process. It can not only be unspeakably dull, but also terrifically difficult to convey to lay readers in a compelling fashion. This fact is recognized by the congressional leaders who fashion these procedures. In a 1987 interview in the *Washington Post,* Rep. Robert Michel, the Republican floor leader in the House at a time when the Republicans had been in the minority for 33 years and had been consistently stymied by Democratic control of the rules of procedure, observed bitterly:

> Nothing is so boring to the layman as a litany of complaints over the more obscure provisions of House procedures. It is all "inside baseball." Even among the media, none but the brave seek to attend to the howls of dismay from Republicans over such esoterica as the kinds of rules under which we are forced to debate. But what is more important to a democracy than the method by which its laws are created?
>
> We Republicans are all too aware that when we laboriously compile data to demonstrate the abuse of legislative power by the Democrats, we are met by reporters and the public with that familiar acronym "MEGO"—my eyes glaze over. We can't help it if the battles of Capitol Hill are won or lost before the issues get to the floor by the placement of an amendment or the timing of a vote. We have a voice and a vote to fight the disgraceful manipulation of the rules by the Democrats, and we make use of both. All we need now is media attention, properly directed to these boring but all-important House procedures.

Michel's lament is one that has resounded throughout history, but it contains some assumptions that we may need to examine. One assumption is that journalists understand the procedural machinations of Congress but choose not to write about them because the topic is not sexy. This may well be the case inasmuch as process is not an intrinsically riveting topic and is always trumped by personalities. Some print journalists do make a dutiful effort to explain to their readers both the substance of legislation and its processing, but even the most diligent coverage, except in such specialized publications as the *Congressional Quarterly Weekly Report* or *National Journal,* tends to suffer from an ailment traditionally attributed to diplomats who have spent too much time in small Third World countries. It is called "localitis" or going native. Its central postulate is that the dusty capital to which you are accredited is not only the center of the universe, but also a cynosure to which the eyes of all the world should be drawn. The trains of reasoning that flow from this are two: 1) The world is keenly aware of the minutest perturbations in this tropical backwater. Reports on it, accordingly, find an eager, informed and attentive audience; or 2) one has a duty to report the goings-on even if the world doesn't care.

Journalists who cover Capitol Hill often find themselves in one of these two frames of mind, and the coverage that results reflects the distinctive problems of both. Often you have coverage in which the journalist clearly considers it unnecessary to provide much context. There is an assumption here, which may well be correct, that the only people who read congressional reporting are sophisticates who are well up to speed on the difference between a continuing resolution and a cloture vote. So we are told that the House will be voting on Thursday on a budget reconciliation, and we may even be told that the reconciliation contains a tax cut and a reduction in the amount of money for entitlement programs such as Medicare. But we are rarely informed about why these disparate pieces of legislation are combined in a single bill, or who invented the reconciliation or how its use has changed over the years.

This type of coverage typically uses such breezy but unhelpful catchphrases as "stopgap spending measure" to mean continuing resolution or "tax and benefits package" to mean reconciliation bill. The word "markup" is commonly used but almost never defined so as to inform the reader or viewer that it is the process by which a committee rewrites a bill in light of evidence produced in the hearings on the bill. Providing both context and periodic explanation may not do much to enlighten the general public or make them feel less estranged from the process, but it will at least reduce the information costs of the attentive publics who read the *New York Times* and the *Washington Post*.

There is yet another assumption that needs to be examined in regard to journalistic coverage of Congress and that is that journalists themselves understand the process. It is not a desirable situation when the journalists know but do not tell; it is quite a bit more troublesome when it appears that the journalists don't tell because they don't know.

I do not mean to suggest that there is widespread ignorance of the legislative process on the part of political reporters, but one recent example from the "MacNeil/Lehrer NewsHour," a program that is surely the gold standard of political journalism, at least hints at a problem. On Oct. 20, 1995, the focus of the influential PBS program was the battle over the budget in Congress. After correspondent Kwame Holman had extracted some commentary on the reconciliation bill that was being considered by the House and Senate, anchor Jim Lehrer turned to the chief economics correspondent of *U.S. News and World Report,* Susan Dentzer, who explained that the reconciliation bill contained changes in taxes and in mandatory programs. Lehrer then inquired of Dentzer why it is called reconciliation. She replied that "it's an attempt to reconcile the fiscal policy of the nation with the budget targets set forth earlier in the year by both houses of Congress."

Lehrer looked puzzled but replied "OK" and went on with the dialogue. But he was clearly unsatisfied and brought up the subject later on the show when columnists Mark Shields and Paul Gigot analyzed the news of the week.

Shields seemed eager to discuss the tactical maneuvers of the week between the White House and Congress, but Lehrer interrupted him by saying: "You know, I had to ask Susan just now, OK, tell me again what reconciliation means. I have a hunch I was asking on behalf of myself as well as the audience."

Mark Shields: Sure—
Jim Lehrer: I've got a hunch that an awful lot of people don't know what it is.
Mark Shields: Well, this is the whole ball game all wrapped together.
Jim Lehrer: OK.
Mark Shields: This is welfare. This is—.
Jim Lehrer: All—

Mark Shields:—Medicare. This is tax cuts. This— everything put together. The president is going to veto it. All right. The president has to veto it.

At that point the dialogue broke off into the political cut and thrust that the panelists really wanted to discuss, leaving Lehrer still looking puzzled on his own and on behalf of the viewers who cannot have been greatly enlightened by Shields on the subject of reconciliation. Perhaps the best statement of the evening had been supplied earlier in the program by Rep. John Kasich, R-Ohio, chairman of the House Budget Committee who expostulated: "Reconciliation? That's the dumbest word I've ever heard in my life—you'd think it was something the Catholics do on Saturday."

Whether it is because journalists avoid discussions of procedure because their editors or producers shun such things, because they perceive that the public is uninterested or because they themselves feel uncertain about their own grasp of the process, the effect is to keep the public in the dark. In conjunction with other factors, the perception on the part of citizens that the process is unknowable and hence beyond their influence contributes to a sense of alienation and estrangement from politics.

There is no better example of Beltway insiderism than the manner in which the legislative process is infused with needless complexity by politicians and shunned or sloppily reported by many journalists. The combined effect of the two is to hoodwink the people by a priestly class speaking a language as incomprehensible to ordinary citizens as Ge'ez, the liturgical tongue of the Ethiopian church. The effect is exclusionary and what is created is an information environment inhospitable to the uninitiated.

There is no implication of a vast conspiracy between politicians bent on evading accountability and lazy, complacent and uninformed journalists. There is, however, a very clear implication that both groups, in their own way, aren't really doing their jobs very well.

Some politicians have actually attempted to come out from behind the procedural smoke screen and put themselves on record. A recent vote in the House in which the $270 billion cut in Medicare was the subject of a separate vote rather than having it concealed in the 1,949-page reconciliation bill was an important step in the direction of accountability for which Speaker Newt Gingrich and Budget Committee Chairman John Kasich deserve credit.

On the journalism side, the willingness of Jim Lehrer to resist the temptation of journalistic insiderism and to play the role of the uninitiated citizen is commendable. The team assigned by the *New York Times* to cover Congress occasionally comes down with bouts of localitis, but an informed reader can usually figure out what is going on. There has also been a heroic effort by some radio journalists to use the medium least conducive to presenting process to give listeners a sense of what is going on at a time of legislative hyperactivity. Peter Kenyon, Elizabeth Arnold and Cokie Roberts of National Public Radio have been especially dutiful in trying to speak in the clear.

A more open and comprehensible process and a more diligent media are no panacea for the ills of contemporary politics. There are structural problems that need attention, but a little openness will certainly help because, as Dahl has written, it is not surprising that an incurable political system makes voters feel powerless over their government.

A citizenry that felt connected with the manner in which its laws were made was, for Alexis de Tocqueville, a critical element in American democracy. He wrote in 1835: "The American learns to know the laws by participating in the act of legislation; and he takes a lesson in the forms of government from governing. The great work of society is ever going on beneath his eyes...."

The vigilance of the press over the policy process should not be limited only to policing the perks, probing the plunder and pillorying the philanderers. It should extend to presenting the process, even at the expense, sometimes, of the juicier stories. To stand up in front of a camera and say, "This is the way the process really works," or to take a three-sentence detour in a 750-word story to tell readers why politicians are taking cover behind an order of procedure rule, might not be electrifying journalism. But it might leave the citizen slightly less befuddled and less cranky.

Ross K. Baker is professor of political science at Rutgers University and a regular contributor to the Philadelphia Inquirer's commentary page.

Part II
Media on the Hill

2

Evolution and Revolution

Timothy E. Cook

In the waning weeks of the election campaign, the party's leader took a gamble. After sophisticated research on polls and focus groups, he committed himself to taking precise actions on specific issues in the first 100 days after he took office. He won an unexpectedly strong victory, handpicked a new team and took office with a stirring defense of his governing philosophy. A frenzied 100 days of activity, marked by many televised press conferences, ended with a round of celebratory interviews with top reporters and finally a nationally televised speech.

Prior to this year, one would have presumed such a description to be about an American president, or at least the prime minister of a parliamentary regime. But since the spring of 1995, it will be most familiar as what Newt Gingrich undertook to become speaker of the House and then what he did once he was there.

At first glance, Gingrich appears to have occasioned a revolution in the speakership: he seems to look outward to the rest of Washington, even to the rest of the country, rather than inward to his congressional colleagues. In the language of Congress, he uses an "outside" stategy, not an "inside" stategy. He claims to borrow at least as much from presidents—FDR, Eisenhower, Reagan—as from previous congressional leaders. Gingrich has certainly transformed the speakership; he wields far more centralized power than any speaker since the "czar rule" days of Thomas B. Reed and Joseph G. Cannon. The present speaker also places greater reliance than his predecessors on publicity, with a sophisticated and proactive media strategy playing a key role in governing strategies. Making news and communicating to the public may be at the core of Gingrich's notion of leadership. A leader, he has said, should first and foremost be "a visionary definer, agenda setter and value articulator for the community."

Gingrich may well love to blast the news media for what he has called a "disinformation" campaign against him. But only Richard Nixon could rival Gingrich in being simultaneously a creation of the news media and its harshest critic.

Why is publicity so central to Gingrich's speakership? One explanation is that the media were intrinsic to creating the path that he took to power. Another explanation is that there is an established tendency among Republicans, partly because of having been in the minority in Congress and partly because of their greater internal cohesion, to use the news to discuss their agenda. But neither of these possibilities suggests why, now that Gingrich is the leader of a Republican majority in the House, he persists in a political strategy so focused on the media.

I am more persuaded by a third possibility: that in a political system where power is fragmented among a number of players, a media strategy is indispensable to getting something done and one of the few effective ways of focusing the attention of otherwise distracted political actors. Media coverage can set the agenda, put a spin on particular issues, raise the stakes of opposition to a given program and create the perception of a public mood that is beneficial or detrimental to a cause. Although Gingrich's media strategy may seem like that of a president, it is more correct to say that today all ambitious political figures—presidents, members of Congress, bureaucrats or interest-group representatives—have to deal aggressively with the news media in order to get something done.

The media speakership that has emerged under Gingrich is revolutionary, but it is based partially on an evolutionary process that has already occurred in the House. Gingrich came to leadership by an unconventional route. Traditionally, aspiring congressional leaders cultivated friendships, worked diligently on committees, "got along and went along" and gradually rose through the ranks. But Gingrich, when he first took his seat in 1979, paid little attention to his committee assignments or to short-term legislative accomplishments. He was already consumed with the big picture. Early in his term, Gingrich instructed Republican leaders that they should avoid accommodation and instead exploit the possibilities on the floor to go to the people and make a case against the Democratic majority. He noted his aim in a 1979 interview: "The Congress in the long run can change the country more dramatically than the president. One of my goals is to make the House the co-equal of the White House."

One vehicle was a caucus, the Conservative Opportunity Society, formed with other junior Republican House members in the early 1980s. Emerging out of a battle against a tax increase that President Reagan reluctantly urged in 1982, the Conservative Opportunity Society staked a claim as "movement conservatives" and denounced the stances of Speaker Tip O'Neill, D-Mass., and even, occasionally, Senate Majority Leader Robert Dole, R-Kan., whom Gingrich once excoriated as "the tax collector of the welfare state." And they found new ways to get their messages out—the one-minute speeches that allow any member to give a short discourse at the start of the legislative day and the special orders that allow one or more members to go on at length at its end. With C-SPAN broadcasting live gavel-to-gavel coverage, with around 200,000 viewers tuning in at any time, Gingrich proclaimed that "that's not a bad crowd.... This is the beginning of the ability to have a nationwide town meeting."

Who knows if this strategy would have gone very far if it had not resulted in an explosive response in 1984 from Speaker O'Neill, who denounced Gingrich on the House floor and was subsequently reprimanded by the presiding officer. The resultant publicity gave Gingrich far more attention than he would have acquired from C-SPAN alone. This news bounce may have been what interested Gingrich, rather than national town meetings, judging from what he said to the *Washington Post* in 1985: "Think of me as a backbencher who used to work very hard trying to figure out how I can articulate something in a flashy enough way so the press can pick it up."

Once on reporters' radar screens, Gingrich continued to meet the demands of the news media for dramatic, terse, argumentative statements. In 1988, Hedrick Smith provided an admiring profile in *The Power Game* that outlined Gingrich's approach: "Be splashy; be original; be outrageous; be strident; even be inflammatory. He is a classic show horse, more interested in promoting confrontations and ideas than in passing legislation." Nevertheless, Smith concluded, "Brash video politics...put Gingrich on the political map."

With a background like this, Gingrich's narrow election as minority whip in mid-1989 sent shock waves through Washington. Gingrich made no apologies for his paltry legislative record or for his inexperience at counting votes. Instead, his victory was quickly judged by Minority Leader Robert Michel as a sign that Republican members "want us to be more activated and more visible and more aggressive." In other words, the strategy that had brought Gingrich to a leadership position—an "outside strategy" of deliberately speaking to the world beyond Capitol Hill—would not be dropped upon gaining inside power but would be a key part of his new job.

The Gingrich approach grew out of precedents developed by both Republicans and Democrats in Congress. By the '80s, the outside strategy was hardly unfamiliar to Republicans. When the first television-minded president, John F. Kennedy, was elected in 1960, the Republican leaders in Congress—Sen. Everett Dirksen and Rep. Charles Halleck—began a regular series of televised press conferences that journalists dubbed the "Ev and Charlie Show." In the House especially, where the majority leadership can and increasingly did deftly control the schedule and thereby the agenda, outnumbered Republicans sometimes had little choice but to go public in attempts to force their concerns and proposals into legislative debates.

From the '40s through the '60s, Democratic Speakers Sam Rayburn and John McCormack paid little attention to the national press as a whole—apart from their cursory "speaker's briefings" that outlined the legislative day. Their successors, however, adopted higher profiles, usually in order to catch up to the increasingly media-centered presidency. Thus, when President Nixon withdrew from press conferences and offered instead nationally televised speeches from the Oval Office, Speaker Carl Albert began to request equal time for Democratic responses. O'Neill, who followed Albert, played a major role in initiating television coverage of House floor proceedings in 1979 after members had concluded they could not keep up with the president without video feeds from Capitol Hill. In the aftermath of Ronald Reagan's election, O'Neill found that the strength of the conservative coalition made his parliamentary powers less useful. Accordingly, he made a more concerted and successful effort, with the help of an aggressive press secretary, to reach the news media and a large public audience. The next speaker, Jim Wright, began his tenure in 1987 with a flurry of lone-ranger initiatives that were perfectly suited for legislating through and with the media. And finally, Rep. Thomas Foley's, D-Wash., speakership was marked by the increasing integration of newsmaking into governing, as party leaders gathered each morning for a variant of the "line of the day" meeting, which the Nixon White House had pioneered and the Reagan White House had perfected, to both manage the news and set political priorities.

But leaders' media strategies, which were in part responses to the White House, were also aimed at the Congress itself. In a huge institution such as the House, legislators must turn to the news as one way to find out what the Congress is up to. When they do so, they find plenty of legislators and press aides anxious to inform them. All members now have the potential to get into the news, particularly if they can lay claim to a swing vote, a key constituency or special expertise. With most House offices now containing a full-time press secretary at taxpayers' expense, ambitious and policy-minded individual members' media strategies can and do become central components not merely of getting re-elected, but of exercising power in Washington.

Since congressional leaders are usually deemed to be more authoritative sources, they can counter such initiatives by backbenchers—but only by going public themselves. Party leaders on both sides of the aisle are thus trying to play catch-up ball, not only with the media operations of the president, but also with those of their junior colleagues.

While Gingrich may represent the apogee of media-mindedness in congressional leaders, he has built his strategy on developments that were already well along under his Democratic predecessors. The Gingrich marriage of media and governing strategies is only the latest in a series of such unions. The current speaker's pairing of the two may be more effective than those of his predecessors, but that says as much about Gingrich's political situation as it does about his own skills or priorities.

Speaker Gingrich has benefited greatly from both the discipline of his party and its domination of both houses of Congress—two elements that were lacking for his Democratic predecessors. Barbara Sinclair, the finest scholar of House leadership, has noted how in the early '80s Democratic leaders were asked to perform two crucial but often contradictory functions: passing legislation and "keeping peace within the family." With a fractured majority, Democratic leaders had to perform a balancing act between the two that usually produced cautious action at best. By contrast the new Republican majority is, for now, more united.

It is a coalition of more senior moderates who are anxious to govern at last and junior conservatives, who are pursuing an ideological program. And it is probably not much of an exaggeration to say that Gingrich's aggressive media strategy—and his constant attempts to keep "on message" by what he himself has termed "maniacal, relentless repetition"—may be crucial to holding this coalition together and reminding its members of the costs of dissent or inaction.

But if this majority coalition begins to founder, Gingrich's current media strategy may serve Republicans less well. Gingrich's take-no-prisoners approach has resulted in singular personal unpopularity in the polls. And as past studies of members and their staffs have shown, media strategies are better for getting an issue onto the agenda than for getting something accomplished. The press secretary to a Republican leader, who spoke to me in 1984, put it this way: "Before legislative action, you want exposure, you want to generate public attention and public interest. Then you get to actually legislating and putting the pieces of the puzzle together, and you *don't* want it; you've got everything cranked up and then a story in the *Post* can kill you.... Sometimes it becomes a matter of shutting off initiatives: don't go to the press and don't generate an initiative and they won't be there."

Eventually Gingrich may face a dilemma: having mobilized the media to focus attention on his agenda, he must reckon with the prospect that someday they might pay attention to him at a time when he finds their coverage less useful, if not counterproductive. The speaker, for example, terminated his initial practice of holding televised daily press conferences—in part because they blurred his focus. Ultimately, maneuver as he might, Gingrich's control of his own coverage remains incomplete.

And whether Gingrich's media strategy solves the problems of governance in a confused and dispirited political system is also an open question. Working with the news media pushes politicians to accommodate the media's expectations of what makes for a good story. Gingrich admitted as much in an interview with *USA Today*: "Part of the reason I use strong language is because you all will pick it up.... You convince your colleagues to cover me being calm, and I'll be calm. You guys want to cover nine seconds, I'll give you nine seconds, because that is the competitive requirement.... I've simply tried to learn my half of your business."

Fitting journalists' expectation for clear-cut, decisive, vivid, terse and visual news pushes legislators toward particular priorities, issues, actions and processes. Speaker Gingrich's penchant for speaking to the nation through the media deepens the division between inside and outside strategies, between deliberation and public relations, between building a majority for legislation and "selling" issues to the news media and thereby to the public.

Republican Rep. Steve Gunderson, R-Wis., a key ally of Gingrich in the 1989 whip election, aptly noted last spring, "What matters to the public is passing the titles of the bills. The fights on the floor don't matter." As Gunderson went on to say, the strategy may be "brilliant," but it may result in policy outcomes that are closer to "accidents." Gingrich's marriage of governing strategy and media strategy, in short, may produce an outcome that is ironic for someone who professes to think in the long term: a quick fix with uncertain results.

Timothy E. Cook is professor of political science at Williams College. He is author of Making Laws and Making News: Media Strategies in the House of Representatives *and is currently writing a book on the news media as the fourth branch of government.*

3

Getting Out the Message

Newt Gingrich

On exposure:
 If you're not in the *Washington Post* every day, you might as well not exist. —*Vanity Fair,* July 1989

On his press coverage since he's been speaker:
 First of all, the Washington press corps is essentially liberal. Second, the Washington press corps spent most of the last 40 years knowing Democrats in Congress, and a lot of people had to scramble to start figuring us out. Third, we are a genuine revolution, and nobody has figured it out yet.

On getting out his message:
 So my attitude toward the press right now is that I have a message that I am going to get out. I'll get it out by maniacal, relentless repetition, and occasionally some of you will pick up parts of it. But I don't rely on the elite media to carry anything. I mean, I just keep working away at what I am trying to get done. —*USA Today,* June 7, 1995

On democracy and the threat of decay:
 Unfortunately, modern news media contribute to the problem because they do not cover progress as well as decay. They pander cynically to the basest tastes and look upon any declarations of belief in God or the unique American as corny and unsophisticated. They devote copious airtime to reporting the details of the O.J. Simpson case but can't seem to figure out how to cover the most important stories for the entire human race.... —*New Perspectives Quarterly,* March 22, 1995

On the news media and conservative values:

We've had a long history of a rough-and-tumble news media.... The problem has been two things in recent years. One is that you do have a lot of people who grew up as a sort of counterculture, anti-Vietnam war, critics of the American system, made their name during Watergate, and that entire wave of reporters and editors are now fairly senior, and they tend—much like a college faculty—they tend to select out people who share their worldview to hire and promote. So you have a bias in favor of a sort of great society counterculture model.

...The second is that an awful lot of them live in a very tiny enclave. They talk to each other, they ride on the campaign bus, they gather in the press room, they don't spend much time sympathetically going out and listening to...ordinary working class Americans who believe in American civilization, a general phrase which used to mean normal.

—From a Q & A session at the Heritage Foundation appearing in *The Baltimore Sun,* Nov. 21, 1994

On religion and reporting:

Reporters and editorial writers routinely practice Christian-phobia.

—UPI, Sept. 8, 1995

On getting media attention:

The number one fact about the media is they love fights...You have to give them confrontations. When you give them confrontations, you get attention; when you get attention, you can educate.

—*Mother Jones,* November 1984

Newt Gingrich, R-Ga., is Speaker of the U.S. House of Representatives.

4

Speed Over Substance

Ann Compton

The couch potato, that creature who has taken up residence in so many American homes, channel surfing and blind to the world around him, is also gaining a foothold in the ranks of broadcast reporters covering the U.S. Congress of the '90s.

The broadcasting technology that blanketed Capitol Hill in miles of fiber-optic cable has helped to transform work for the men and women who report on Congress. Caught in the daily competition among correspondents, many do not even seem aware of the changes that are certainly shaping the news we report in ways that privilege speed over substance. The video of Speaker Newt Gingrich marching into a news conference brandishing a golf club, while the president is AWOL on the first tee, makes quick theater for the evening news—but it doesn't explain the latest impasse on the budget. Shrill sound bites from the floor condemning the use of American troops in Bosnia may be attention grabbing, but they shouldn't take the place of a full account of how Congress would cut off funds for such a military mission.

I was chairman of the Radio-Television Correspondents Association in the mid-'80s when the technology boom hit the Hill. Our networks, with the help of the established congressional bureaucracy, wired virtually every corner of the working rooms and spaces of the Capitol building (and six giant congressional office buildings) with fiber-optic cable. The cables, which ran to hub rooms, could pump pictures from a dozen sites back to our network headquarters at the same time. The screens of our television monitors were soon filled with plenty of action.

At the same moment, the Senate offered broadcasters a big new space for their working "gallery." A remodeling produced electronically sophisticated working booths for every one of us, each wired with four or more television monitors, nearly a dozen telephone lines, fax machines, even an electronic bulletin board for the instantaneous posting of late-breaking events. We could surf the congressional action without leaving our seats. These isolated but wired working booths became indispensable command decks from which reporters strayed only at their peril, lest they miss a major development.

The politicians began to change too. The Old Guard that opposed television on the floor of the House and Senate in the '70s was retiring. The newcomers to Congress were media smart, computer literate, fax crazy and eager for "face time," especially with network cameras. Capitol Hill was suddenly short of press conference space, so tiny interview rooms were improvised and the lawns outside the House and Senate became electronic Hyde Park corners.

Gone was the old routine of shoe-leather reporting, trolling hallways outside caucus rooms and dining rooms to catch a quote. Gone too from the isolation booths in which we worked was the sense of community we reporters had all shared when we operated out of one big common area in the old press gallery, where rumors and hunches grew and flourished.

At first, print journalists were not subject to these changes. Their gallery had not been renovated since the telephone replaced the teletype. On serious issues like the budget, committee chairmen still made a beeline to the print reporters who wanted every decimal point explained, every nuance spelled out.

But newspaper reporters, who usually cover the beat without the presence of producers, technicians, researchers and occasional interns, could not be everywhere all the time. So they too began to rely on watching one key hearing televised on C-SPAN while waiting for congressmen to return their phone calls on other issues.

Finally this year, with the new Republican leadership in the House and Senate, one of the oldest reporters' institutions began to die. We used to be ushered in to the hushed well of the Senate chamber, or the inner sanctum of the speaker's office, just before the day's floor session was to begin. Here we saw the leadership up close and personal and asked anything we wanted to about strategy, scheduling or reaction to the latest comments from the White House. Those intimate moments went public in January, when Speaker Gingrich began holding his daily sessions before cameras and microphones. The Senate majority and minority leaders often did the same. But for reporters, the incentive to be there was not the same. To hear amid the growing throngs of reporters that now crowd every press event, it was almost safer to listen back in the quiet of the gallery. To beat the wire services and CNN with the headlines for your editors, it was easier to be sitting right next to your phone.

Sophisticated communications technology has taken the "I-was-there" authenticity out of Congressional coverage. And what's worse, so many of us are lulled into the sense that by seeing everything, we know everything. We don't. And our reporting has begun to show it.

Ann Compton, a founding member of the Center's National Advisory Committee, covered Congress for ABC News in the late 1970s and mid-1980s. She now reports from the White House Press Room.

5

Getting on the Radar Screen

Rachel B. Gorlin

MEMORANDUM

TO: Congressman Fred Wildebeest
FROM: Deep Spin
RE: Communications Strategy Going into the 1996 Election, or How You're Going to Learn to Stop Worrying and Love the Media

We face a daunting challenge in organizing the media strategy for your campaign to be the next U.S. senator from the state of Narnia. As we all know only too well, no politician running in 1996 is going to get a free ride from either the Fourth Estate or the voters. We'll need to use all the tricks of the trade to get you as much coverage as possible based on your congressional incumbency (though we should be careful to avoid your being referred to as "Congressman"—"Fred" is preferable—and being seen as an "incumbent," which is, as you know, a dirty word in the minds of the electorate).

Bear in mind that our polling shows a third of the voters have never heard of you at all. In addition, of those folks who say they've heard of you, most know absolutely nothing about you. This gives us an opportunity, in essence, to create your identity as the campaign goes along. But there is real peril involved if we don't define you before your opponents do. That's what media coverage is all about: creating an image of you that will attract 50.1 percent of the electorate. We must not only generate more coverage in all news media than you've been getting, we must also get a different kind of coverage.

Let's face it, the "substance" stories you're used to being covered in as a member of Congress with a relatively safe seat ("In Rotary Speech, Wildebeest Urges Foreign Aid Cut") are ignored by most people, especially those whose votes are up for grabs in a Senate race. Political/policy coverage is still important to money people, political players and some of our base. But as much as we can, we will need to go over the heads of traditional political reporters and get onto talk radio and TV, the World Wide Web and the newspaper feature pages to create the impression we want Narnians to have of you.

All the earned media—and by that I mean all the free coverage in bona fide news outlets—must dovetail with our paid media, which won't start until August for the November general election. Until then, we're relying primarily on the press, broadly defined, to deliver our message to the voters. That needn't be as scary as it sounds if we do this right.

As we make media a greater priority in all parts of this operation, we have to remember that we can only exert partial control at best over your coverage. Our chances of maximizing our control depend on being able to meet the media's needs, as well as being able to frame our issues so they make news. Let's keep the following points in mind:

1. Never miss a casting call.

First and foremost in the "media friendly" make-over of the Wildebeest operation, we need to start taking advantage of reporters' periodic on-deadline "casting calls" for a member of Congress who sounds knowledgeable about the breaking news of the day. (For example, giving a sound bite on the congressional prospects of federal earthquake relief after the "big one" in California.) You may know nothing about a topic, but with some good, fast staff work you could become an instant expert—for a few sentences at least, which is usually all that matters. This is crucial to the day-in, day-out success of the guys who cover D.C. for Narnia news organizations and who don't have access to, say, Bob Dole or a cabinet secretary. Reporters almost never have a hidden agenda at times like this. They're not looking to make trouble; they just need a quote from a "knowledgeable" source and the congress member who makes the time for them gets the airtime or the ink. Of course, we won't ever ask you to do an interview on a topic that does us no good, like adultery or term limits.

Before the Senate campaign, you blew off these potential opportunities with alarming regularity; I've heard enough grumbling from the regional press corps to know it's cost you with them. They end up having to go to other members of the congressional delegation who just don't give as good sound bite. The next time we set you up to answer a casting call, don't look at it as a waste of your precious time that could be better used fund-raising or legislating or whatever. Think of it instead as an investment in future coverage that you need to move your message. And, in weighing the minutes it takes to prep for and actually have this kind of chat with either a print or broadcast reporter, just think how much it would cost to buy the broadcast time or print space you'll get in the piece. Believe me, the time spent on the interview is worth it.

2. *Spinning turns straw into gold and issues into messages.*

Issues and policy are the votes you cast, the bills you introduce, the ideas you push. In and of themselves, they don't elect anyone to anything. A campaign for an office or a legislative outcome is affected by message. And policy becomes message when it's spun—and not until then.

In the past, with your safe seat, we haven't usually needed to do much spinning. Have we cared what someone thought about your vote on, for example, some obscure trade bill? If someone had had a question, we would have copied the description of the vote itself from *Congressional Quarterly* and sent it to him. But a lot of people would care now: the unions considering your endorsement, your opponents in both the primary and the general election, various business groups with conflicting interests. That means the media are more likely to pay attention, which is, of course, both good and bad news.

In other words, we would need to spin that vote on the obscure trade bill as a measure that would bring more family wage jobs to Narnia—before your opponents turn it into a payoff to special interests. Ideally, you'd speak on the floor during the debate on the bill, complete with a chart detailing state Department of Economic Development estimates (which we can get if we have enough time) on the amount of money and number of jobs it will bring to Narnia. Charts are always good for floor debates and for other events we want the media to cover. Where a visual element will help get you on TV, other props work, too. The memory of Rep. Jolene Unsoeld on the floor with her Exxon Valdez oil-slicked rock from about five years ago will long linger in my mind, though I doubt she actually said anything memorable.

Back home, we could find a business that could potentially benefit from the trade bill becoming law and hold a news event there. It would be particularly good if the business were telegenic—so say the bill could result in trade opportunities for the new ostrich-breeding ranches that are springing up around the state. In addition to the excellent TV potential, the ostrich ranchers could be a good hook to get off the pages of the newspapers' front section (which swing voters tend not to read) and into a more useful part of the paper like living (gals), business or sports (guys).

3. Animals make great visuals.

Animals are a guaranteed must-cover for TV and print photographers. Haven't you noticed that Gingrich is always appearing with critters or remains thereof, in which category I include that gargantuan dinosaur skull in his office? (Now I didn't say animals guaranteed favorable coverage.) The pictures get on the tube and in the paper. So next time we set up an event or a photo-op with native fauna, don't laugh. The only exception to the rule that animals are good press is anything that could create a problem with the anti-fur and humane society people. Specifically, if that mink farm at the state university invites you to visit again, I don't care whether the state's pelt industry is an economic miracle, you're not going.

4. Celebrities can get you covered.

Although I'm a fanatic about staying on message, I'm an utter advocate for flexibility when it comes to opportunities to get the message out. For example, a year and a half ago when we got a last-minute invitation to a D.C. press conference with Ted Danson about extending the ban on off-shore oil drilling (an effort about which Narnians care a lot and on which you've been a leader for years), you couldn't be bothered to rearrange your schedule to fit Ted in. This year, I would cut my wrists on the Capitol steps if you blew off a chance to appear with a popular celebrity on one of your own issues. It's guaranteed coverage on TV news all over the state.

5. Plan to be spontaneous.

Don't forget, you have had success with spur-of-the-moment media opportunities. Look at all the coverage you got with that one-minute speech inspired by your disgust with the recent spike in gas prices. Not only did our satellite feed of the speech itself get good TV play all around the state (all Narnians care about the cost of gas), but it was picked up by CNN, two of the networks and NPR. Even better, it was a more-than-one-day story when the energy secretary had to answer questions about "congressional demands that she investigate price fixing in the oil industry." That was your idea, so let it never be said that you don't know how to do this. From now until Nov. 5, we need about one media opportunity a week based on serendipitous spontaneity.

6. Good quotes aren't always safe quotes.

One of the reasons national reporters particularly like interviewing you is that you will often say just what you think, without mincing words and trying to find the "safe," inoffensive quote. Occasionally this has gotten you into trouble, usually with the House leadership. But in taking stock of your media profile, I think it's been worth it for you not to play it safe. It's not as though the quotes—like that line in the *New York Times* about the corrosive role of money in politics or years ago saying that members wanted then-Speaker Jim Wright to resign— were setups for your opponents to use against you.

Now that we're in campaign mode, I hope you won't interpret any of this memo as a bid for excess caution in what you say to reporters. Taking calculated, well-considered risks is, in fact, integral to what we're doing, and you're the focal point of that. Also, we know you're incredibly good at it. It gets you that sound bite on TV (even sometimes when, from a strict news judgment standpoint, you may not warrant it). And when it comes to print, you need to keep making those dry, pithy observations to Adam Clymer so *The Narnian*'s editors have to wonder whether your coverage in the *Times* means they should be doing more on you in their crummy paper.

7. Packaged right, substance does sell.

The legislative centerpiece of your candidacy is your "Better Jobs for Narnians Act," an omnibus job training voucher/tax credit/increase in the minimum wage/education improvement bill. None of these ideas is really new, but your bill knits them together in a way that is both credible and comprehensible to the general public (folks know that if schools don't improve, businesses will leave, for example). It's also of interest to the media now simply because you're a candidate for the Senate and because you're known as a serious legislator, not a press hound. As you know, we've already been working on a major media push around the introduction of the bill next month. Bill introductions are notorious news nonevents, but I think we can overcome that with some ingenuity.

First, I think we need to fly in Narnians whose lives would be changed by aspects of the bill—a young fast-food worker, a timber worker whose job has vanished and is struggling to pay community college tuition so he can become a medical technician, a small-business owner who wants to expand her firm but can't get the capital. These people would be covered by the regional press corps and the wires, which is what we need. We can do pretaped radio interviews with them and feed them out to stations all around the state. In fact, we can even do a satellite feed from the House Recording Studio, since none of this is, according to House rules, campaign related. (It's legislative!)

The bill will automatically go up on the Internet, as all legislation introduced in the House now does. I've been amazed to hear from other offices what kind of impact this can have. While we're on the subject of cyberspace, the campaign can also put material about the legislation up on their web site. But we'd better make sure the junior staff in the D.C. office don't get this assignment, or they'll spend all their time surfing the net and get no constituent mail answered between now and Election Day.

During the next congressional recess (excuse me, "district work period," as it says on the calendar from the whip's office), we can do a repeat of our Washington dog-and-pony show on the bill in the major media markets around the state. Even if TV and the papers have already covered it from D.C., they'll have to do another story if you show up in town. It would be even better if we could get local dogs and ponies for each media market.

We'll also book key TV and radio talk shows for you and a couple of those locals who'd benefit from the bill. Newspaper editorial board meetings focused on the bill are another component of this state swing.

The "Better Jobs Act" is a great hook to start sharing with the editorial writers who will eventually be doing the endorsements. It's always better to have a focus when going in to see editorial boards; that way, you control more of the dialogue and prevent meandering conversations about things that are decidedly off message, notably higher taxes (which *The Narnian,* you'll recall, supports) and hydroelectric power rate reform (an old standby at several Narnia papers along the river, pro and con, depending).

A slightly controversial op-ed piece on this for the *Washington Post* would be great if we can find a way to do it. They won't use something that's strictly parochial about Narnia's needs, but we could use our state's particular situation to weigh in on the national budget debate: the current budget proposals from both parties don't deal with the real problems faced by real families beyond the Beltway and could make them a lot worse. Your bill is held out as an example of a piece of a solution. It would take some work but could really be worth it. This kind of exposure in print leads to national (and regional) broadcast invitations, not to mention that we could use the piece itself as a mailing to our supporters and donors.

Unfortunately, your House committee assignment, Appropriations, isn't ideal for hearing opportunities to push legislation into the public eye. Oversight committees with hooded witnesses, victims of some sort and tabloid topics produce coverage galore, but neither you nor the Appropriations Committee has gone in much for such sensationalism. If we worked hard, there might be some opportunity to get coverage on job training and education when the secretaries of Labor and Education testify about their budgets. However, I think we'd have to get the secretaries' answers to your questions wired in advance, otherwise total dullsville.

8. Learn to deal with reporters.

I know you think that a lot of reporters—especially ones who work for Narnia news organizations—are jerks, or worse. Some of them are, while some of them just work for jerky editors. A few are a lot smarter than they seem on the surface, which is important to keep in mind. Right now, we need them all—in the interest of getting you as much decent coverage as possible. Acting on your overly broad and only partly accurate perception that they are jerks won't help. In addition, as you've heard me say before, journalists are like dogs—they sense when you don't like them or are afraid of them, which is when they move in for the kill. Don't think I'm saying these guys and gals are your best friends—it's certainly appropriate to be on guard. You are at the point, however, where it would be a very good investment in your future to do some schmoozing—drinks and dinner, rather than a meeting in the office—with key reporters and columnists both in D.C. and back home. We can go through the list and decide with whom you could profitably stand to spend quality time.

And that's not all for social occasions. When you get the inevitable invitations to the Radio-TV Correspondents Dinner and the Washington Press Club Foundation's Congressional Dinner, where reporters invite their sources to sit at the tables their news organizations buy, you need to go and be charming.

And we need to start doing weekly get-togethers (okay, press secretaries tend to call them "gang bangs," but don't let that put you off) with the Narnia reporters in D.C. when Congress is in session. First thing in the a.m. early in the week is good, with coffee and danish (it will improve coverage because reporters will go anywhere there is food). The agenda is simple: you give them a mostly on-the-record heads-up about what's likely to happen in the course of the week, with an emphasis on stories with a local Narnia angle. Let's try one in the next two weeks and see if you think you could handle it on a regular basis.

Ultimately, you need to achieve a zen-like serenity about your relationships with members of the Fourth Estate: you'll have more control over what they do if you go with the flow rather than chafing at the bit when you have to deal with them. The paradox of this is that once you get into that mode, you can direct and sometimes even change the course of the flow itself.

About reporters who burn you (an unfortunate inevitability, but rarer than you fear), there are only three hard-and-fast rules about how to deal with these situations: namely, don't lose control, don't do anything in public and don't go over a reporter's head to complain about a story—and certainly not unless you've complained to the reporter himself. Another cardinal rule, except in extremely rare situations, is to let the staff do the dirty work here (Note: Mario Cuomo's marathon pre-dawn phone calls to reporters were not a constructive exception).

As a candidate you should strive to remain serene, on message, focused and above the fray. As Oscar Wilde once put it, "We are all in the gutter, but some of us are looking up at the stars."

Rachel B. Gorlin, a Capitol Hill and political campaign veteran, writes regularly from Washington for the Boston Globe*'s Sunday "Focus" section.*

6

Toward Civic-minded Media

Bill Bradley

On the media and American values:
   I am saddened on occasion when the media, and politicians themselves, convey that politics is mean, cheap and dirty; that what we hold in common as Americans is somehow less than what we harbor in our hearts and minds for ourselves as individuals. I have never believed that.   —Excerpted from a statement in Newark, N.J., Aug. 16, 1995

On the media and citizenship:
   Alongside the decline of civil society, it is a sad truth that the exercise of democratic citizenship plays, at best, a very minor role in the lives of most American adults. Only 39 percent of eligible voters actually voted in 1994. The role formerly played by party organizations with face-to-face associations has been yielded to the media. Local TV news follows the dual credos, "If it bleeds, it leads; and if it thinks, it stinks," and paid media politics remains beyond the reach of most Americans. When only the rich, such as Ross Perot, can get their views across on TV, political equality suffers.
   ...We need a more civic-minded media. At a time when harassed parents spend less time with their children, they have ceded to television more and more of the all-important role of storytelling, which is essential to the formation of moral education that sustains a civil society. But too often TV producers and music executives and video-game manufacturers feed young people a menu of violence without context and sex without attachment, and both with no consequence or judgment. The market acts blindly to sell and make money, never paus-

ing to ask whether it furthers citizenship or decency. Too often those who trash government as the enemy of freedom and a destroyer of families are strangely silent about the market's corrosive effects on those very same values in civil society. When a factory closes in a small town, or an employer finds a loophole in the law to escape pension responsibilities for its workers of 20 years, this too is an assault on civil society. The answer is not censorship but more citizenship in the corporate boardroom and more active families who will turn off the trash, boycott the sponsors and tell the executives that you hold them personally responsible for making money from glorifying violence and human degradation.

—Excerpted from "America's Challenge: Revitalizing Our National Community," Englewood, N.J., Feb. 12, 1995

Bill Bradley formerly served as the senior U.S. Senator from New Jersey.

7

Making News, Making Law

Ronald D. Elving

President Bill Clinton held his first bill-signing ceremony just 16 days after being inaugurated in 1993. The bill before him was the Family and Medical Leave Act, the product of nearly a decade's legislative gestation. Clinton's staff was so eager to publicize the event that it summoned the media to the Rose Garden on the same Friday the bill cleared Congress, despite the White House supply room's lack of new pens bearing Clinton's name.

The Friday evening news programs looked in on the signing ceremony briefly, and many Saturday-morning papers put it on the front page. But the big play in all media for that cycle was the fresher and juicier story of Kimba Wood, the New York judge whose nanny arrangements had just cost her the chance to be the nation's first female attorney general. For the advocates of family leave, the irony of being upstaged by a woman with child-care problems was painful but predictable. For the romance between this legislation and the news media had long since lost its bloom.

When the issue had first emerged in the mid-1980s, the coverage had been uniformly friendly. The idea was simple and loaded with human appeal—the kind of "kitchen table" story news managers always seem to want. But after the issue had been reduced to a bill and run through the legislative mill—repeatedly, with all the attendant alterations—"family leave" lost its cachet. In the congressional reporters' galleries, the bill became an old story (and therefore an uninteresting one) even as it gradually gained the votes it needed to pass.

The family-leave story offers an unusually vivid case study of how media attitudes toward a bill can cool over time and how that fading of enthusiasm can complicate a bill's fate. It is also useful in demonstrating how the media may miss, or at least fail to communicate, much of what is really going on when a bill becomes a law.

The relationship between family leave and the news media began warmly. The idea of allowing time off to care for new babies or sick family members was a natural for feature treatment, for heartfelt prose and pictures of moms nuzzling infants or sitting anxiously at a hospital bedside. Much of the early press attention came from columnists such as Judy Mann of the *Washington Post,* who adopted the cause early and wrote about it often. There were also op-ed articles by activists (such as Steve Max of Citizen Action), child psychologists (among them, Edward F. Zigler of Yale and Sheila Kamerman of Columbia) and feature stories about Harvard Medical School professor T. Berry Brazelton, who had popularized the subject of "bonding."

But the most effective early journalism on the subject may have been the stories about Lillian Garland, a receptionist at California Federal Savings and Loan whose job loss in 1982 prompted a protracted legal battle. Cynthia Gorney wrote an account of her case from Los Angeles that ran in the *Washington Post* in April 1984. In July, Tamar Lewin of the New York Times used the Garland case to frame a long inquiry into the legal issues of leave policy.

Garland had filed a claim against her employer using a California state law enacted in 1978 to protect women's job rights in pregnancy-related cases. After a complex series of legal maneuvers that reached all the way to the U.S. Supreme Court, her claim was allowed to stand. And at each stage of that legal process, the Garland case stirred flurries of press attention that, in turn, raised the issue's visibility on Capitol Hill.

It was the original court ruling against Garland in March 1984 that led to Gorney's story in the *Post* the following month. That ruling had also inspired a spate of meetings involving members of Congress from California and members of the Congressional Caucus for Women's Issues (CCWI). One of those involved was Rep. Howard Berman, a first-term Democrat who, as a California state legislator in the 1970s, had sponsored the law now at issue in the courts. Berman and some of his colleagues wanted to introduce a bill that would make his California statute a federal law, amending other federal laws as necessary.

"It all started boiling about the same time," recalled Rep. Pat Schroeder, the Democrat from Denver who would soon be intimately involved. "The Garland case got an awful lot of ink at about the same time there were a lot of stories about pediatricians looking at bonding."

Berman and Miller and the other Californians were eager to proceed with a bill to protect new mothers, but they were persuaded to hold off. A group of feminist lawyers, led by Donna Lenhoff of the Women's Legal Defense Fund, insisted that a "mommy only" bill would do more harm than good, in part by discouraging the hiring of women of childbearing age. Lenhoff found an ally in Schroeder, the most senior woman member of Congress and co-chair of CCWI.

Early in 1985, Schroeder introduced the first family-leave bill. It covered mothers and fathers, applied to family illnesses as well as to new babies and covered all businesses with more than five employees. It provided for up to 26 weeks of leave with a continuation of benefits; but after lengthy internal debate, the sponsors and supporting organizations agreed not to require the continuation of pay.

On the day Schroeder introduced this legislation, she had three bills to "drop in the hopper" at once. She visited the House clerk to check on the numbers available. The most appealing coming up was HR 2020, and Schroeder arranged her three bills so that family leave would get that number. Just as she imagined, there would soon be editorials that spoke of "a farsighted bill" and a "clear vision of the future."

When the average member puts out press releases, they get ignored by all but the local reporters from the member's own district. But Schroeder's verbal flair (it was she who dubbed Ronald Reagan "the Teflon president") could generate media attention better than nearly any other House Democrat without a chairmanship or a leadership post. When family leave won a critical House vote shortly before Mother's Day in 1990, Schroeder said, "We finally did something more than just chocolate and cards."

But while Schroeder was a godsend for her bill's publicity, she was also hazardous to its immediate legislative health. Within months of the bill's introduction it was becalmed in the House Education and Labor Committee. The reason was that Schroeder had surprised her party leadership with a vote against a bill to require worker notification prior to plant closings, the top legislative priority for organized labor and its allies in the Democratic hierarchy.

To revive family leave, it was necessary to reintroduce it the following year with several amendments negotiated by labor lobbyists, a new co-sponsor and a new bill number. The new co-sponsor was Rep. William L. Clay, D-Mo., a senior black member of Congress with a labor background and little if any affinity for the press. The new number was the less eye-catching HR 4300. Another news conference was held, this time with Schroeder's ceding to Clay and the feminist groups' ceding to union representatives. The bill had a new round of hearings, won committee approval and was made in order for floor action by the House Rules Committee. But the 99th Congress (1985-86) would end without a vote on family leave. The blocking of the bill at this point was accomplished by a combination of legislative process and political forces that might have made an interesting news story, but in the absence of a vote there was no peg to hang it on.

On the Senate side, the father of family leave was Christopher J. Dodd, a Democrat from Connecticut, who, while divorced and childless, had a lively interest in family issues. He sponsored the first family-leave bill in the Senate in 1986 and reintroduced it in 1987, after the Democrats had taken control of the Senate in the most recent elections. His party's return to power gave Dodd, now in his second term, the chairmanship of a subcommittee on the Senate Labor and Human Resources Committee. Dodd could now schedule hearings on his own bill, and he did so in February 1987, opening the hearing by waving a clipping of a Linda Greenhouse story from the *New York Times* that made mention of his interest in family leave.

Dodd from the beginning understood the interplay between legislation and re-election politics, and he did not underestimate the importance of favorable publicity to re-election politics. After conducting that first hearing in Washington, Dodd directed his staff to take the show on the road. He subsequently held field hearings in a dozen cities that spring and summer. In Boston, the hook was a special appearance by Sen. Edward M. Kennedy, D-Mass., and his partially disabled son, Patrick. In Los Angeles, cameras came out to see the actor Richard Dreyfuss and his wife. But even in Chicago, with no celebrities, the hearing brought out both major newspapers and the local TV and radio stations as well.

"We got good press wherever we went," recalled Rich Tarplin, the Dodd aide who handled family leave for years. Dodd was always conscious of the political task known as spin control. In Tarplin's phrase, it was "framing the debate as greedy big business against families in crisis" and countering opponents who would frame it as "mom-and-pop store vs. yuppies who would use leaves for vacations."

But while hearings serve to create an atmosphere and advertise the virtues of a bill, they can only serve as an introduction. At some point, the bill itself has to move.

Reporters had begun to notice the opposition to the family-leave idea, which came from a variety of business groups such as the U.S. Chamber of Commerce, the National Federation of Independent Business (NFIB) and an ad hoc group called the Concerned Alliance of Responsible Employers (CARE). The business opposition began to organize in the winter of 1985, after the appeals court had overturned the first ruling in the Garland case and Schroeder had introduced HR 2020.

The opponents were careful not to attack family leave as an idea or as an employee benefit. They only opposed the notion of a federal mandate that would force businesses to grant leaves. They said some businesses could not survive the dislocation and that all businesses would suffer losses when the leaves were abused. The groups were also at pains to send sympathetic individuals—usually women who had children themselves—to testify at committee proceedings. These included both the salaried lobbyists who worked the congressional offices and the witnesses they recruited to tell how family leave would harm their small businesses.

The groups that opposed family leave never felt that the news media gave their case an adequate presentation. The plight of the small-business owner never made as compelling a story as the distressed family. Nevertheless, the opponents' lobbying succeeded in altering the bill to exclude all businesses with fewer than 50 employees, which excluded about 95 percent of all the businesses in the country (and more than half the employees).

The strong and steadfast opposition of the business groups—especially the NFIB—kept the family-leave bill from getting a floor vote in the House not only in the 99th Congress but also in the 100th Congress (1987–88). Dodd's bill got to the floor of the Senate late in 1988 strictly as part of a package of bills brought out to help Democratic presidential nominee Michael Dukakis campaign against Republican nominee George Bush. Dodd did not have the votes to break a GOP filibuster, and his bill had to be "taken down."

It was not until May 1990 that family leave reached the floor of the House and won, achieving its first (and very nearly last) pinnacle of newsworthiness. Victory in the House brought the bill (HR 770) to the front page of the *Washington Post* and the *Los Angeles Times* (and to extensive play on an inside page of the *New York Times*). The vote also received prominent mention on the major broadcast networks, whose news programs are still the main source of news for most Americans and whose agenda affects that of other journalists. In the weeks that followed, editorialists lined up for and against the bill.

The coverage tended to emphasize that the 237 votes for the bill were not nearly enough to override an expected veto. The coverage saluted the contribution of New Jersey Rep. Marge Roukema, the bill's leading Republican exponent in committee. But little was said in the press of the crucial coalition between the feminist advocates and such social conservatives as the U.S. Conference of Catholic Bishops in support of the bill. More than 40 Republicans had voted for the bill in the House, many of them following the lead of conservative Rep. Henry Hyde, R-Ill., the legendary leader of the anti-abortion movement. Hyde argued that women entitled to keep their jobs after childbirth were more likely to carry to term. Journalists' failure to explore the crucial contribution of this odd alliance to the passage of the bill typifies the left-right analysis that dominates political journalism and misses the often-critical crosscurrents.

The momentum held in the Senate, where Dodd struck a deal with Sen. Christopher "Kit" Bond, R-Mo., scaling back the force of the bill and recruiting several new co-sponsors from Bond's side of the aisle. The Senate Republican leader, Bob Dole of Kansas, conceded that he did not have the votes to sustain a filibuster this time around. Then he surprised the advocates by suddenly allowing the bill to pass without a roll-call vote, a technique used by Senate leaders who know they cannot prevail on a recorded vote, and who also know that by conceding defeat they drain most of the drama and confrontation out of the floor action.

This scoreless game displeased the bill's opponents, who wanted to see who their real friends were. It also reduced the moment's news value in the minds of many editors. The voice vote on June 14 received far less coverage than the House vote had in May. Two weeks later, Bush vetoed the bill. As this was expected, it occasioned even less news coverage than the Senate vote had. The override attempt in the House came nearly a full month later and fell so far short that the story barely made print. Insofar as it was a story, it played as another success for Bush and his veto pen, a team that remained undefeated. The big story that month was still Bush's decision to drop his "no new taxes" pledge and include revenues in the budget-deficit reduction deal he was hammering out with Hill Democrats. By August, Iraq's invasion of Kuwait had moved the media focus once again to the Middle East, where it would stay for most of the next nine months.

In the next Congress, the 102nd (1991-92), family leave would again be passed and vetoed by President Bush. In the fall of 1992, the Senate would override that veto, but the House would fall far short. In the first weeks of 1993, with a new president anticipating a bill, the 103rd Congress would once again pass family leave.

But none of these subsequent efforts would be accorded much notice, and individual reporters seemed numbed by the repetition of committee process and floor debate. "I think people just got incredibly tired of the arguments," noted Jill Zuckman of the *Boston Globe* (who in 1993 was covering the bill for *Congressional Quarterly*). Having managed to hook their editors and producers on the story once, reporters found its news value deflated in each successive cycle.

The relationship between family leave and the media never wilted entirely. But the sense of urgency required to sustain media interest seemed lost after the first failure to override in 1990.

Some among the bill's advocates were surprised at the way the coverage fell off in the 1990s and disillusioned with the altered tone of reporting. The bill had been "watered down," the stories said. Even Schroeder used the phrase in explaining why it was "hard to continue to be enthusiastic" about what had once been her own legislative baby.

"The hot moment of press support was in '86 and '87," recalled Andrea Camp, a staff person for Rep. Schroeder. "As for attention, we probably peaked in '90 with the first House floor vote. After that people thought the story was in the past." Jackie Ruff, another Dodd aide who worked the bill, said she could remember no "outrageously negative press coverage," but became "frustrated at the tone of 'oh well, here it comes again.'"

Still, even the disillusionment of the press may have had a hand in advancing the bill. Lenhoff, the lawyer who shepherded family leave from concept to Rose Garden, liked to say that every time a news report referred to the bill as compromised, the purpose of the compromise was realized and reinforced. Every time the bill was said to have been weakened, it strengthened the supporters' bid for new votes. "It hurt us to see it referred to as 'watered-down,'" she would say. "But it helped with the members [of Congress]."

The law took effect Aug. 5, 1993, and follow-up stories have come in clusters on the first and second anniversaries of that date. Like the debate over the bill itself, these anniversary stories have been long on anecdote and rhetoric—pro and con—and generally short on objective analysis.

The attempts made to date to measure the law's effect have tended to undercut the central theses of both the supporters and the opponents. Surveys by the Business Roundtable, the Labor Policy Association, the Labor Department and several universities have found the law causing little disruption for business—in part because it is little used. One California survey found less than 1 percent of all employees taking family leaves. The surveys note that covered employees are either unaware of the benefits of the law or unable to take the time off without pay. But there have also been anecdotal reports in the *Wall Street Journal* and the Associated Press of employees abusing the law for frivolous purposes.

Some see the low incidence of use as proof that the opponents' fears were groundless, others as proof the law itself was unnecessary. But the survey evidence showing sparse public awareness of the law probably also reflects the relatively sparse media attention it has received since enactment.

Reporters are routinely prevented from telling much of what they know about an institution such as Congress. They are not restrained by censorship or editorial policy but by a lack of time, a lack of space or a lack of interest. Because the legislative track has so many stops, scheduled and unscheduled, reporters have trouble differentiating them for editors, who are inclined to say, "Call me when they finally do something." In the absence of a recognizable news peg—a vote on final passage or an attempted veto override—news organizations rarely expend resources on a pending issue in Congress.

And yet it is in these passages of time—when nothing appears to be happening, between hearings and committee votes and floor votes—that the real story of a bill unfolds. When a reporter spends the time to explore these areas, the result is typically dismissed as "inside baseball" or the product of a reporter "going native." In March 1991, Paul

Taylor of the *Washington Post* wrote an unusual story about the status of the family-leave bill at the start of its seventh year in Congress. It dealt with the interplay between members behind the scenes and the maneuvering necessary to steer a bill from committee to the floor. It played inside on the paper's page of news about the federal bureaucracy. When a bill actually wins floor passage and commands prominent play, the space or time available is usually constrained. Thus a dimension such as the role played by Rep. Hyde on family leave in the House may get short shrift.

This is important not only as a cause of discouragement among journalists but as a cause of dissatisfaction with government. One reason the public is unhappy with its leaders is because it knows so little about what they actually do. Not all of this is the citizen's own fault. Granted, the average American is not consumed with curiosity about Congress on a daily basis. But when the interest is there, the information is too often hard to find.

Members come to the Capitol with full heads of steam, insistent on the ideas and interests they individually represent. When they collide with each other, their differences are apparent and often highly combustible. The news media generally portray this vividly. But conflict is only half the congressional story. In time, most members come to realize they cannot accomplish anything as individuals. They need to find friends, to forge coalitions. This requires them to talk to each other, to listen and to bargain. Their success in this process of compromise determines whether they will transcend their conflicts to accomplish anything.

In this latter realm, the process of compromise, the techniques of conventional journalism are less readily brought to bear. We cannot see the process as well, if at all. It has less immediate appeal to readers and viewers and so, logically enough, it has less appeal to editors and program directors.

The fate of family leave was determined not by the repetition of unchanging arguments, which bored us all, but by years of subtly shifting relationships, most of them hidden from our view. Majorities were assembled one vote at a time. The negotiations that underlay each change in the bill's particulars involved internal struggles between elements of the supporting coalition.

All this, too, is human drama worth retelling. The larger story, however, the one that might have remained more compelling, was a far more time-consuming story to pursue. Ultimately, the family-leave case study has this lesson for the news media: with the increasing importance of Congress in national life, the time has come for a reallocation of resources in the news business that will give reporters the time and space they need to tell the public what it needs to know about our national legislature.

Ronald D. Elving is political editor of Congressional Quarterly Weekly Report *and author of* Conflict and Compromise: How Congress Makes the Law.

8

Behind the Noise on the Floor

Donald Rothberg

The issue that drives the coverage of Congress is legislation. But the latest evolution in congressional coverage at the Associated Press is that we are doing much more on the interaction between Congress and the other branches of government.

When I went up to the Hill as head of the Associated Press Senate staff in the late '70s, we had very distinct staffs: a Senate staff and a House staff. We also had regional reporters who covered news of interest to particular geographic parts of the country. We had people who covered the Senate and only the Senate, so that if a piece of legislation originated in the Senate but then went over to the House, someone else covered it. But after a few months of looking at the way things worked, it seemed to make more sense to combine the staffs.

Today, we've gone beyond the time when the story is simply what someone says during debate on the floor. If you look at our stories on any major bill on the floor, there will be some representative quotes from the debate on both sides, but there will be much more of an effort to try to explain to the reader why this bill has reached this point. We ask, "What's really at stake here? Is this a challenge to Clinton's foreign policy? Is there some political motivation behind this action if, say, Bob Dole, who is running for president, is sponsoring a resolution on foreign policy?" We have to try to get away from the stock stories that might have run years ago, in which it was basically, "Senator so-and-so said this...." The AP and other press institutions have made the decision that what's really important is what is behind the noise that's coming from the floor.

The coverage of Congress is also much more intense than it was before the Republicans took control. The Republican victory in the '94 elections clearly changed the way all news organizations had to look at Congress. In the area of foreign policy, I now spend far more time on the Hill than I did when the Democrats were in control and we had a Democratic president. Now there is a challenge to Clinton's foreign policy and, obviously, challenges to budgetary and economic policies. These aren't empty challenges. These are major changes between the legislative and the executive branches, and they are very big news. You wouldn't narrowly define it as politics. These are very different philosophies of what the federal government should be doing. This is Congress attempting to impose its will and the administration pushing for its concept of how the federal government should work. It's really a fascinating confrontation. Suddenly the press corps is finding itself covering a really exciting story.

Donald Rothberg is foreign affairs correspondent for the Associated Press Washington Bureau. He was head of the Associated Press congressional correspondents from 1974 to 1980.

9

Big Picture and Local Angle

Melissa Merson

The chairman of the powerful Senate committee gavels the hearing to order in a process barely changed since the birth of the nation. Before him, the chairman of the Federal Reserve Board of Governors begins to speak, reading the formal, written testimony he holds before him on the mahogany table. The room is packed with staff members, representatives of private industry and reporters. All are hushed, straining to hear the chairman's words. Against a timeless backdrop of huge billowing curtains, polished wood walls, chairs and tables, everyone is focused on the man at the table, whose measured words can raise or lower interest rates around the world.

Off to the side of the room, reporters sit crammed around a rectangular wooden table, listening hard, scribbling on their pads. To the untrained eye, they are totally absorbed in the Fed chairman's words. On close examination, a trained eye would see the difference. The reporters eyes dart from their notebooks to the chairman and then around the press table. Furtively, almost suspiciously, they eye their colleagues. First, a chair squeaks slightly. Then chaos breaks out. A dozen reporters push back from the table. They climb over chairs, knocking some over as they race out the door. Once outside, they madly punch numbers on cellular phones and begin dictating rapidly. Many of them simultaneously work tape recorders, rewinding tape in search of the pertinent quote. Within seconds, the Fed chairman's remarks are around the world. From New York to London to Tokyo, modern technology rapidly moves information that once took weeks if not months to reach distant shores. The significance of this, of course, is that there is little time to absorb and assimilate new information before a new barrage of it arrives. Government units and financial markets worldwide are compelled to respond instantaneously to news with little time to analyze and weigh results and consequences.

This is the reality of journalism on Capitol Hill, where modern communications technology operates in a setting structured by tradition and political protocol. The combination can have unpredictable results, which do not always make for good journalism. The Capitol today is home to four separate press galleries, one each for daily publications, periodicals, photographers and radio/television. The term gallery refers to the upper tier of seats inside the House and Senate chambers. For the press, each gallery consists of a cordoned-off section of the balcony. Access to each of these is limited to those reporters with credentials issued by the appropriate gallery. Each gallery has its own rules, traditions and idiosyncrasies. Each gallery, governed by its members with distant oversight from the congressional rules committees, decides which reporters and photographers are permitted access to the Capitol workspace and to the press tables in congressional hearing rooms. Each gallery also decides who may lay claim to the press releases and printed testimony, produced by Congress in mass quantities each day, which are the currency of congressional life.

Every gallery contains a large working space. Here reporters work under ornate ceiling fixtures and paintings at desks crammed with the latest in computer technology and fax machines. The gallery staff directs a seemingly endless flow of telephone calls and packs press releases delivered from House and Senate offices into bins where reporters can retrieve them. Each gallery is tailored to the needs of its members: radio/TV reporters have sound booths, and print reporters have phone booths for private telephone interviewing. Most reporters have small televisions enabling them to monitor House and Senate floor action and television news, usually cable news networks.

The Capitol has been a fulcrum of tradition and technology ever since Samuel Morse demonstrated his telegraph machine there in 1844. Soon reporters regularly filed news from the Capitol using the telegraph and suddenly, news of Washington became current. Folks heard about events in a timely way, in time to respond if they wanted to influence further action.

Membership in the first congressional press gallery initially was restricted to reporters who filed for daily newspapers. Its members, seeking to maintain exclusivity and to ward off competition, resisted efforts by those who worked for weekly publications or the broadcast media to gain entry. This only slowed the inevitable progress. By 1939, radio correspondents won their own gallery, although it took until 1953 for television to be added to their domain. While radio and television correspondents have their own gallery that caters to their needs, there remains in the daily gallery a sense that newspaper scribes somehow are more entitled to their special space, although wire-service reporters from the Associated Press and elsewhere work hard to keep them humble.

While television reporters were permitted to roam the halls of Congress, they were not allowed to film daily sessions or committee hearings on a regular basis until the mid-1970s. Previously, only important hearings might be televised, and these usually were on the Senate side and at the discretion of the chairman presiding over the committee. In 1973, a trial period permitting live coverage of the Senate was instituted, but it was not until 1986 that there were sufficient votes in the Senate to approve regular television coverage of Senate action.

Today, television coverage of the House and Senate is taken for granted. Frequent film clips of votes or speeches pepper the evening news. The parliamentary processes of the House and Senate are open for anyone, anywhere, to see, and elected officials know it and play to it. They hire image consultants to improve their on-air personae. The bill on the floor does not always seem to be the most important thing.

The story of television coverage illuminates the effects of new technology on both the media's and the public's view of news. Television allowed more information to travel rapidly and allowed more people to react more quickly to current events. Now, when Congress takes action, congressional switchboards often get flooded with telephone calls from citizens eager to voice their opinions. People now react to events well before they have complete information, which can result in distortions of events and reactions that lead to further distortions in public sentiment.

Millions now follow congressional activities on C-SPAN and CNN. Televised coverage of Congress in general has opened up politics to the citizenry, educating the public in ways never before possible. Television also has taken its toll on the legislative process. In the early years, House Speaker Thomas (Tip) O'Neill, D-Mass., irked minority Republicans by ordering the cameras to pan the House floor when they spoke late at night to show the country there was no one in the chamber listening to whoever was speaking.

Regular coverage of the Senate in action required sweeping changes in Senate rules, changes that some think have strengthened the hands of whichever party is in the majority and weakened the minority. Previously, after the Senate voted to invoke cloture, the procedure used to shut down a long debate or filibuster on an issue, there still would be 100 hours of debate remaining. The magnitude of that time block often forced parties to negotiate legislative agreements even after the filibuster was shut down. With television came new rules to speed up the action. Although not quite as dramatic as the basketball shot clock, the new rules called for only 20 hours of postcloture debate, a period of time easily passed without any need for further deliberations.

Television also has influenced relations among members of Congress. In a recent interview in *The Hill* newspaper, Rep. Anthony Beilenson, D-Calif., a 20-year House member retiring at the end of his current term, said that television has changed the House for the worse in that "the more outrageous members are the ones that get the most attention," even if they're not the most important members. "People back home are frustrated and upset when they see some of this stuff on television," he said. "When we were working quietly, off in the distance, strangely, we were doing a better job."

The unforeseen consequences of new forms of congressional coverage also have influenced the ways in which journalists do their work. The passage of time and the evolution of technology have blurred the jurisdictional lines of the press galleries. A newcomer to Capitol Hill might assume that all the reporters in the daily press galleries represent daily publications, but this is not always so. *Congressional Quarterly,* by name not a daily, is an important member of the daily press gallery. *CQ* does have a daily publication in its stable and electronic news products as well, but it is not primarily a daily publication. *CQ* stays where it is because that is tradition, where it always has been. Gallery rules do not call for any ongoing evaluation of evolving media and technology. So while technological progress continues, and traditional media outlets evolve to meet the demand, the credentials process remains steeped in tradition and has changed little over time. There's no movement, say, to provide a separate gallery for electronic media. Nevertheless some who work for electronic news outlets sometimes feel like second-class citizens. And the reporters who work for "real" newspapers are treated better by staff and others who underestimate the wide readership of the new media.

At the same time the periodical gallery is the home of daily publications. The Bureau of National Affairs, Inc. (BNA), a large, employee-owned business and legal publishing outfit that was launched more than 50 years ago by *U.S. News and World Report* and put out on its own a few years later, is one of the largest members of this gallery, with more than 100 members. The most visible BNA reporters on Capitol Hill and in the gallery do not work for periodicals, though. *The Daily Report for Executives, Daily Tax Report* and *Daily Labor Report* all are published daily, yet their staffs work out of the periodical gallery. Commerce Clearing House, Prentice Hall, *Tax Notes* and others all publish daily yet reside in a periodical gallery. Much like the situation with *CQ*, these news outlets are where they are by tradition. Indeed, most periodicals and magazines now have electronic news products and Internet sites, but by tradition they remain credentialed according to their initial print product.

To confuse the situation more, there's the matter of electronic journalism. The world's financial markets are powered 24 hours a day by a continual flow of news from the capitals of the world, and Washington is a key source of business and financial news of global importance. Reporters for electronic news services from around the world flood congressional hearings on banking, budget, commodities, monetary policy and tax. They work at high speed, racing to beat each other to the markets with an abbreviated headline or two made up of whatever words will make the markets respond. They roam the halls of the Capitol in packs. In times of budget crises, annual events in Congress in recent years, they nervously watch one another's every move, sometimes following the other lest a competitor gain some advantage.

Electronic journalists often use the telephone to dictate reports that are edited on the fly by swift editors who move the copy onto wire services that broadcast headlines within seconds and reports shortly thereafter. Within 15 seconds of uttering the words, a reporter's thoughts are around the world. Such journalists do not have the luxury of reviewing their copy or rethinking a story's opening lines. Mistakes are inevitable.

The words fly so fast that some question whether such electronic news ought not be linked to the broadcast galleries rather than print, but electronic journalists, who send news instantly around the world, do not work out of the broadcast press gallery. They work with the daily press.

The speed of the new electronic journalism is such that reporters can cover Congress even though they are physically far from Capitol Hill, in some cases even though they lack congressional press credentials. A reporter without a press pass cannot obtain access to restricted congressional hearings or easily gain possession of hearing documents such as witness testimony statements, press releases and reports. Once, this would have been a crippling disadvantage. Today, however, specialized services geared to the Capitol community make it increasingly easy for reporters and editors denied or given delayed access to the primary materials or living at a distance to write, report and editorialize as if they were within the Capitol complex. Federal News Service provides timely verbatim transcripts of most key congressional events and hearings. Arriving in one's office within hours of the conclusion of a hearing, reporters can write as if they attended the event even if they never set foot in the door. While the distance may strip from their writing the contextual richness allowed by a seat in the hearing room, the reader rarely notices.

Congressional Quarterly, the venerable periodical that chronicles in infinite detail the progress of legislation as it makes its way through the legislative process, today boasts of its Washington Alert service. Much like the legi-slate service owned by the Washington Post Co., Washington Alert provides subscribers, many of whom pay upwards of $20,000 per year or more, access to a sophisticated database that includes pending legislation, political information, congressional testimony, committee reports and letters members of congress circulate on the Hill.

Among the news organizations that cover Congress on behalf of the world beyond Capitol Hill, the juxtaposition of traditional media like newspapers and television alongside new electronic news services has further accelerated the transmission of information, requiring even more rapid absorption and response. Print and television reporters show grudging respect for the high-energy of the electronic press. They display a similarly tempered enthusiasm for the media that cover Capitol Hill for the people who work there. Among the Hill's hometown media, the arrival of new media of all kinds has required old-timers to move over and make room. Upstart new kids on the block always make their elders edgy at first, but it would be impossible not to respect the value provided by speeding up the delivery process. It's as if the newsboy chucked his bike and bought a motor scooter.

Consider *Roll Call,* the newspaper of the Capitol community for 40 years. Initially a weekly, in recent years it has been published twice each week, eagerly awaited by those who work in or in work related to the Congress. *Roll Call* is a newspaper for insiders; it caters to members of Congress and their staffs.

To appreciate its significance, it helps to understand something about the sense of community on Capitol Hill. Contrary to public opinion, most congressional staff work in miserable conditions, crammed into too-small offices where they are expected to work absurd hours for ridiculously low pay. At the same time the public thinks they work in palaces with free food, free valet parking, free banking and free jobs for all their family members. The difference between the reality and the perception is vast and that gap creates a sense of community among Hill staffers.

Roll Call tracks staff members, who come and go with great regularity from Senate and House member and committee offices. In times of budget turmoil, it keeps staff and members informed about impending cuts and changes. For the administrative and other support staffs, including the Capitol Police, it is a source of often otherwise unavailable news.

In the last few years, however, *Roll Call* has faced its first real competition from *The Hill,* a new rival published by former *New York Times* reporter Martin Tolchin. *The Hill* gives *Roll Call* a run for its money. Reporters for *The Hill* go after stories that *Roll Call* eschews, but the upstart's cub reporters lack seasoning and experienced guides to show them around the community they supposedly know. Still, *The Hill* won high marks this year by doggedly pursuing the financial high jinks of former Rep. Enid Waldholtz's, R-Utah, high-rolling husband. Now he's under investigation by a grand jury for check kiting, and she has a lot of explaining to do.

Perhaps the greatest change in the news flow on Capitol Hill in recent years has been the advent of the fax service, rapidly transmitting news across town and across the Hill. Now, what news is not televised instantly all over the world is at the fingertips of those who care before sundown. This means political "spin" or reaction can begin quickly, perhaps in time to influence the evening news. On lesser matters, the jump gives Congress and the White House, as well as lobbyists, time to get their views included in newspaper and other print media reports by the next morning. Where once there was a lag, the reaction to the story now becomes part of the story.

Congress Daily changed the ways news moved across Capitol Hill when it appeared on congressional fax machines each afternoon beginning in 1991. Congress watchers once had to wait until the evening news or the following morning to learn details of activities they followed. But *Congress Daily* (the brainchild of *National Journal,* a prestigious Washington political newsmagazine) is delivered late each afternoon when Congress is in session, providing information early enough in the day that recipients can prepare to influence the morning headlines.

Congress Daily has been followed by dozens of new fax publications, many of them weeklies, that target specific news niches such as health care, telecommunications, or some special-interest area. Financial services, firms and law offices often provide "on-demand" fax news services that cover tax or other legal issues, an outgrowth of the legal memo services that predated the facsimile machine.

The next obvious step in the evolution of news in the Capitol is the shift to the Internet. *National Journal* now is launching *PoliticsUSA*. The new Internet service calls itself the "new World Wide Web source," an on-line community for political professionals. In a joint effort with the American Political Network, which publishes another fax service called *The Hotline, National Journal* aims to provide on-demand news about Congress, the White House and politics, combined with polling data, discussion groups and advocacy information for interest groups.

Clearly, entrepreneurs continue to find ways of repackaging information to exploit emerging technologies and increasingly sophisticated consumer demand. In the history-laden halls of Congress, where reporters plug in their computers in rooms with marble walls and cherubs high above them, this often makes for some interesting combinations. It may be too soon to tell precisely where new technology will take the production of news. Instead of newspapers, Washington commuters may be reading the morning news on portable screens, with front pages updated continuously by the new wireless personal communications technology. The masthead will still wear the traditional gothic type, but imagine a front page that never goes "final." Imagine getting the vote whenever it comes in. The wait won't be long because the world keeps spinning faster. But if the news from Congress keeps coming faster and faster, how will anyone find the time to think about what it all means?

Melissa Merson is manager of the Legislative Tracking Service at Deloitte & Touche LLP in Washington.

10

New Media, Old Messages

Graeme Browning

The Internet is hot stuff on Capitol Hill these days. Every time you look, some member of Congress or presidential hopeful is announcing the advent of a home page, or "site," on the World Wide Web, the graphics-based network-within-a-network that is the cutting edge of the Net.

All this activity seems very hip, very '90s. Shortly after he took office last January, House Speaker Newt Gingrich, Congress' technoprophet, proclaimed that the "old order is gone" from a communications standpoint and that a wholly information-based world is fast approaching. The politically astute in both the Democratic and Republican parties heard his message and have scrambled to get wired. But just how Net-savvy is Congress, really? How well are its members using computer technology to communicate with voters?

Despite the evidence that literally millions of Americans confer regularly through the Internet and despite lightning-like advances in technology that now allow the transmission across the Internet of video, audio and data in a format that's as close to television as computers have ever come, most members of Congress don't seem to have a clue about how to employ the Net to advantage. Except in a handful of instances, politicians in Washington are using the new technology to convey an old message.

Members of Congress want technology to deliver a message in one direction only—from Capitol Hill to the voters. They don't want feedback. There is an appalling lack of real give-and-take going on in the flashy new sites that offices all over Capitol Hill are throwing up daily into that amorphous place called cyberspace.

Take Rep. Ron Wyden's, D-Ore., now a U.S. Senator home page on the Web, for instance <http://www.house.gov/wyden/welcome.html>. Wyden, a Democrat from Oregon, has achieved quasi-hero status in the on-line community because he co-sponsored—with Rep. C. Christopher Cox, R-Calif.—a bill aimed at moderating efforts by the religious right to impose severe government controls on information transmitted via computer networks. Wyden's Web site, however, contains little more than the seals of Oregon and of the House of Representatives—and a large color picture of Wyden grinning cheerily at the camera. Only three items of data are offered: a short note welcoming Internet users to "my page," a list of postal addresses and telephone numbers for Wyden's Washington and district offices, and a series of legislative summaries entitled "Congressman Wyden's Work in Congress."

There's no question that this information is useful. But all of it is already available in printed form and easily accessible at the local public library. Voters who find a trip to the library too burdensome could obtain most of the information over the phone from Wyden's office.

Wyden's electronic dialogue with his constituents could be so much richer than it is now. Unlike the printed page, the Internet is designed to receive, as well as transmit, information. Unlike the telephone, it can do both of these things instantaneously, 24 hours a day, and without human intervention once a host computer is properly programmed. And unlike television, it provides a truly astounding range of information. Searching the Net is like traversing a whole city of libraries, one after another, block upon block. With the advent of new computer programs, it's also possible to watch a video clip or listen to a recording or tune in to the radio along the way.

But many lawmakers on Capitol Hill don't take advantage of these extraordinary features. This could be due, in part, to the Net's relative newness on the Washington scene. The former House Administration Committee established the first pilot project to study the efficacy of electronic mail in congressional offices in June 1993; at the time only seven members of Congress participated in the experiment. Today a little more than a third of the 535 members of Congress have e-mail addresses. Some 78 members of the House and, as of Oct. 20, all 100 senators, have a site on the Web.

More importantly, the bulk of Congress' home pages seems to have been designed without any grasp of the vibrant, substantive, interactive nature of the Internet.

Net etiquette demands, for example, that a home page have the capability of being downloaded off the Internet to a personal computer screen quickly and with a minimum of fuss; about 40,000 bytes of data is usually sufficient for a good site. A number of congressional sites don't follow this rule. Rep. Tillie Fowler, a freshman Republican from Florida, has a home page that contains 238,911 bytes and takes more than two-and-a-half minutes to download on a 14.4-baud modem, which is still the standard among Internet users <http://www.house.gov/fowler/welcome.html>. The home page belonging to Sen. Robert Kerrey, D-Neb., takes almost that long, in part because of the huge color picture of the handsome senator that dominates the site <http://www.senate.gov/~kerrey/>. Even Sen. John D. (Jay) Rockefeller IV, D-W.Va., chairman of the new Senate Democratic Technology and Communications committee, has established a home page that requires a minute to download <http://www.senate.gov/~ rockefeller/>. Regular updating, which keeps a Web site fresh and inviting, also doesn't appear to be a high priority in Congress: many sites contain month-old information, and some haven't been updated for two to three months.

Other sites are just plain boring. The majority of the home pages in the Senate, for example, are no more than electronic reprints of pages from the Congressional Directory 1995–1996, a singularly dull guide to members of Congress published annually by the Government Printing Office <http://www.senate.gov>. In the House, members often mistake eye-popping graphics, byte-heavy color snapshots and folksy text for electronic sophistication. Rep. Joe Barton, R-Texas, for example, has festooned his home page with garish graphics, including strings of barbed wire and hypertext links to such intellectually stimulating locations as the "How 'Bout Them Boys?" home page for the Dallas Cowboys <http://www.house.gov/barton/welcome.html>. Rep. Jim Kolbe, R-Ariz., treats his viewers to an interminable gallery of "action shots" that resemble the family photo album, while a section entitled "Kolbe Speaks" contains a selection of printed speeches and press releases <http://www.house.gov/kolbe/action_shots.html>. And then there's Rep. Lamar S. Smith, R-Texas, whose home page includes an item entitled "How to Contact the Member," which could have several meanings if you think about it <http://www.house.gov/lamarsmith/welcome.html>.

Democrats and Republicans suffer equally from Net ineptness, but Republicans in leadership positions in the House recently demonstrated that they can muster up tons of technological sophistication when the situation demands. When research for this essay was being conducted at the end of October 1995, the home page for the House Republican Conference—in actuality, the House Republican caucus—consisted of only three texts: a "House Republican Plan for a Better American Future," from May 1995; "Speaker Gingrich's Address to the Nation," dated April 7, 1995; and a link to a home page explaining the flat tax proposal introduced by Majority Leader Richard K. Armey, R-Texas.

As of Nov. 14, the day the impasse between the White House and Congress over budgetary issues brought all but the most essential federal government functions to a halt, the Conference's home page sported a whole new look. The headline at the top of the page proclaimed, "No More Excuses. No More Washington Gimmicks." Underneath were hypertext links to essays on such topics as "Why will the president veto reconciliation?" "Republicans keeping their promises," and "White House out to scare veterans." Somebody on the Hill had obviously been burning the midnight oil next to his or her computer.

The cloud of congressional Web disasters has a silver lining, however. When Washington lawmakers "get it" on the Internet, they really get it. In the House, for example, Rep. James M. Talent, R-Mo., provides viewers with links to an electronic database of congressional voting records searchable by zip code <http://www.house.gov/talent/welcome.html>, while Rep. Anna G. Eshoo, a Democrat who represents California's Silicon Valley, has a home page notable not only for its appealing design but also for its hypertext links to Net-based political discussion groups <http://www-eshoo.house.gov/>. And Rep. Vernon J. Ehlers, R-Mich., a former physicist and congressional second-termer whom Gingrich tapped to overhaul the House's computer system, is the only House member to offer electronic excerpts from his speeches, called "audio clips" in Internet parlance <http://www.house.gov/ehlers/welcome.html>.

On the other side of the Hill, Sen. Charles S. Robb, D-Va., has put audio clips—as well as the Internet's bountiful information resources—to spectacular use <http://www.senate.gov/~robb/>. Sen. Patrick J. Leahy, D-Vt., links his page to a Web site where viewers can "sign" an electronic petition aimed at convincing Congress not to regulate the Net <http://www.senate.gov/~leahy/>. And Sen. Barbara Boxer, D-Calif., offers KidsLink, a list of "interesting Web sites for kids," which includes a digital library for schoolchildren, hypertext links to information about various children's issues and a listing for an electronic crisis hotline "for children in need of help" <http://www.senate.gov/member/ca/boxer/general/>. Inexplicably, no other member of Congress provides this important service via the Internet, where a growing number of youngsters now spend their off-hours.

Ironically, the best Web site yet devised for a member of Congress belongs to Bob Dole's campaign for the Republican presidential nomination <http://www.dole96.com/>. Dole, a Republican and the senior senator from Kansas, has a personal Senate home page that is as ho-hum as any other, but his campaign page includes just about every technological marvel currently available for use on the Internet.

Dole fans who want to hear the great man speak the next time he's in town or who want to volunteer as campaign workers need only click on the image of their home state on an electronic map of the United States. Presto! A list of campaign offices in that state, local primary and caucus schedules, and endorsements by local political leaders appears. Prospective contributors can fill out an interactive form located in another section of the site, and the campaign will bill them by mail for their pledge. The "Dole Library" offers up press releases, speeches, photos, audio and video clips, weekly updates on the progress of the campaign, and links the viewer to a searchable database of Dole's voting record and speeches in Congress. And Net surfers who prefer to mix play with their politics can use the two-way programs in "Dole Interactive" to design, and print, their own Dole campaign posters and personalized pro-Dole postcards; test their knowledge of Dole trivia; and download screen savers and desktop images for their home PCs that portray a fiercely gesticulating Dole against a background of either "Colorful Sky," "American Flags" or "White House."

Dole was roundly criticized this past summer for failing to follow suit immediately when three other Republican presidential contenders—Sen. Richard Lugar, R-Ind., Sen. Phil Gramm, R-Texas, and former Tennessee governor Lamar Alexander—announced the establishment of Web sites for their campaigns. There were whispers on Capitol Hill that Dole was shying away from the Internet because he was too old to comprehend it. When the Dole campaign unveiled its site in early October, however, the whispers faded away like smoke.

Clearly, the Internet has uncharted potential to foster new realms of political exchange. The key to the realm lies in interactivity. If members of Congress really want to know what their constituents think about the day-to-day issues of government, they have the power to reach out instantly through their computer keyboards for those opinions. Political dialogues can be carried on through e-mail, of course, but electronic polls, discussion groups, questionnaires, mailing lists, petitions and even games will elicit a public response just as quickly and effectively.

It's debatable, however, whether many members of Congress really want that kind of close relationship with voters. That so few lawmakers have ventured out onto the Internet via an e-mail address, and that even fewer still have established Web sites, says a good deal about the level of comfort they and their staffs have with communicating with constituents electronically.

Some of this discomfort is sheer technophobia. Many longtime congressional aides, some of whom arrived on the Hill before the advent of electric typewriters, are frightened by computers. But their bosses aren't much bolder. Older lawmakers in particular are alarmed at the prospect of one-on-one computer-based dialogues with their constituents, said Robert S. Walker, R-Pa., chairman of the House Science Committee and a key Gingrich ally, in a speech on the Hill last May. "But the growth of technology means that politicians now have to react to our culture instantaneously," he added. "How we're going to handle that is something I'm not real sure of."

Many Washington lawmakers have argued in the past that the Internet community hasn't yet reached critical mass and thus doesn't merit serious political attention. But the pool of Net-active citizens has grown much larger in the last year than anyone inside the Beltway anticipated. A Nielsen poll released in early November concluded that 24 million North Americans regularly use the Internet in some way, and 18 million of those people also use the Web. This is a far cry from the figure of 10–15 million regular on-line users that lobbyists often bandy about on the Hill.

Now, as they say in Washington, you're talking real money. Market research by both Nielsen Media Research and the research division of O'Reilly & Associates, a well-regarded Internet publisher, indicates that the average Internet user is younger, better educated and in a higher salary bracket than the average head of an American household. Equally important, Internet users, particularly those aged 18–29, are consistently more likely to vote than non-Internet users, according to a recent study by the Times Mirror Center for the People & the Press. This last statistic speaks volumes to campaign managers who have watched their candidates lose close races because of low voter turnout. "The people who use the Web were the swing vote in 1992," Tom Gibson, a member of the Wexler Group, a heavyweight political consulting firm in Washington, told me earlier this year. "Those are the people you want to reach in 1996."

Gingrich, the cyberspace cheerleader, would nod his head knowingly at that statement. But don't expect to engage him in a little on-line chat about the subject of a wired electorate: his official Web site includes only a bare minimum of information, and he has been known to ignore his e-mail.

Graeme Browning is congressional correspondent for National Journal. *She is author of the forthcoming book* Electronic Democracy: Using the Internet to Influence American Politics.

Part III
Beyond the Beltway

11

Getting the Whole Truth

Brian Lamb

C-SPAN is, at heart, a simple journalistic concept—the television camera as an extension of the private citizen. Our goal is to give individuals a front-row seat to national debates on policy questions. Our most important task, by far, remains our original one—daily gavel-to-gavel coverage of congressional floor debates.

Ironically, however, Congress has actually restricted citizens' ability to watch its deliberations on television in two ways: by limiting what the cameras installed in the Capitol can show and by enacting legislation that has caused cutbacks in the distribution of C-SPAN telecasts of the House and Senate.

In short, one of the obstacles to full coverage of Congress on television is Congress itself.

Since congressional television's inception in 1979, House and Senate video has been produced solely by government technicians who distribute their product to the media, including C-SPAN. Strict rules govern the pictures they produce from the two chambers. This year, however, a flurry of activity suggested there might be a relaxation of the restrictions Congress places on its telecasts.

The activity was sparked by letters we sent after last November's elections to incoming Speaker Newt Gingrich and Senate Majority Leader Bob Dole. The letters proposed that Congress change its rules and allow us, and other media, to televise live from the chambers with our own cameras.

C-SPAN was quickly joined in the effort for greater access by the Congressional TV Correspondents Association and the "big four" news networks. Across the country, editorial writers urged Congress to allow the public a full view of its debates.

C-SPAN viewers—regular watchers of Congress—were alerted to the issue through news coverage and joined in the debate. A national survey of the C-SPAN audience reported that 75 percent favored giving C-SPAN control of the cameras that bring congressional telecasts into their homes. Many viewers also said they generally wanted to see even more of their national government—more coverage of committee hearings and more coverage of the day-to-day activities of their representatives and senators. As one viewer put it, "Your cameras should be everywhere except the bathrooms."

Immediately upon receipt of our letter, Sen. Dole issued a press release promising he'd "take a serious look at anything that increases public access." However, we heard little from the Senate again on the issue.

The action was more sustained in the House, although it has yet to produce significant changes in the telecasts from the floor. Speaker Gingrich asked Michigan Congressman Peter Hoekstra, a second-termer with close ties to the new GOP leaders, to head a task force looking into the issue of private media cameras. Maryland's Steny Hoyer co-chaired for the Democrats. In March of 1995, the task force asked the five networks that regularly cover Congress (ABC, CBS, CNN, C-SPAN and NBC) for a camera proposal. Delivered in May, the document called for permanently placing up to four media cameras in the House chamber; they would be manned by a rotating pool of the five networks' technicians. The congressional task force has yet to respond.

A short-lived experiment with the House television cameras in spring 1995 demonstrated Congress' resistance to change on this issue. The experiment began when Speaker Gingrich, who controls the broadcast system under House rules, directed technicians to widen their camera shots and present a more realistic picture of Congress.

The change was immediate and dramatic. Suddenly, visual images of the House that had been virtually static for a decade and a half had movement and texture. As their representatives spoke, viewers could see reaction shots from other members; they could watch as members rose from their seats and walked to the rostrum to deliver their remarks and, for the first time ever during legislative debates, television cameras caught scenes of the visitors' gallery and of House members using their electronic voting cards to cast their votes—sights normally seen only by those who visit the House in person. Television viewers could see more of the legislative process—the debate, the side conversations, the voting—for themselves.

A small group of House members from both sides of the aisle immediately decried the new camera angles. Thirty Republicans sent the speaker a letter stating they were "uncomfortable" with the changes. They were unhappy that some House members might appear on camera yawning during speeches or be caught reading newspapers.

Their protests spilled into the news media and Speaker Gingrich was called upon at press briefings to explain his colleagues' complaints. Within 10 days, the internal critics won out; House camera operators were told by Speaker Gingrich to return to near-routine. "House Cuts Candid TV Floor Shots" read the headline in *Roll Call,* a Capitol Hill newspaper.

The protest by a few members aptly makes the case for media cameras in the chamber. Clearly, the technicians had felt the heat from individual members who believed they had been caught in a too-candid moment. And the pressure will always be there, as long as the camera operators covering Congress earn their paychecks from the institution.

Early in his tenure, Speaker Gingrich told Capitol reporters his "bias was in favor of the cameras being allowed to show the country much more of the House." But the speaker also acknowledged that, like any leader, he is subject to the consensus of the people he leads. Whatever his own views, Speaker Gingrich has not yet persuaded a sufficient number of his House colleagues that full television access to the floor is in the best interests of the institution.

We believe the institution—and its members—can survive the media's complete depictions of its debates. After all, C-SPAN and other media have had their own cameras in congressional committees for nearly two decades without causing controversy. And for an institution worried about its public image, we would argue that increased openness might help build public confidence in Congress.

Just as Congress has limited what can be televised in its chambers, it has also acted in ways that serve to limit the number of citizens who see what does get televised. A law passed in 1992—the Cable Television Consumer Protection and Competition Act—actually reduced the available audience for the House and Senate.

Two provisions of the law caused the damage—"must carry," which guarantees free channel space on a cable system for any local broadcaster who demands it, and its near-twin "retransmission consent," which allows popular broadcast channels to negotiate payment for a channel on a cable system.

Both provisions said, in effect, that any programming produced by a federally licensed broadcast station had first right of access to local cable systems—and, therefore, was more important, relevant and useful than programming produced by C-SPAN or any other cable network.

In telling operators which programming services must get preference on their systems, Congress intervened in the cable marketplace. The law's authors hoped to serve the public interest by emphasizing local programming. Instead, the law had the effect of encouraging lucrative new business opportunities for large, well-established commercial broadcasters. It also inadvertently caused serious carriage problems for the two public-service networks cable television had created—C-SPAN and C-SPAN 2.

Prior to the bill's passage, C-SPAN and C-SPAN 2 were on a trend of long-term growth. When Congress decided that local broadcasters should get first access to cable systems, it put the squeeze on systems with limited channel space. Those operators were forced to make tough choices about how to allocate their remaining channels. One result: 6.8 million homes had their C-SPAN or C-SPAN 2 service reduced, or even eliminated—almost 10 percent of our customer base.

For example, in January 1994, seven months after the bill took effect, 120,000 homes in downtown Chicago lost prime-time telecasts of C-SPAN and C-SPAN 2. Instead, the new law gave these inner-city Chicagoans their fourth PBS channel, duplicating their programming choices, and a home-shopping channel broadcasting from suburban Tinley Park, Ill. C-SPAN has just now, in the fall of 1995, returned full time to the system. The system hopes to have C-SPAN 2 restored by the time of next summer's Democratic convention.

In January 1995, 118,000 cable customers in the Portland, Ore., area lost C-SPAN 2 for a broadcast station from Salem—47 miles away. The particular station didn't broadcast for years until "must carry" made its license a much more valuable commodity: whatever it aired would have to be carried on local cable systems. The station was purchased and programmed by the fledgling Warner Brothers Television Network.

Citizens in Alamogordo, N.M., lost C-SPAN entirely for nearly two years. There, our programming was replaced by a religious broadcasting station—their second such choice—piped in from Roswell, N.M., 118 miles away.

As cable technology advances, channel capacity has increased; systems that were forced by the '92 law to cut back on C-SPAN are slowly restoring our service. C-SPAN has also fought the constitutionality of "must carry" by joining forces with other cable networks in a federal suit. The courts currently present the best hope for repeal of this ill-conceived provision. Congress' latest telecommunications overhaul—in conference committee as this goes to press—is silent on "must carry."

Since its creation by the cable industry 17 years ago, C-SPAN has been a model to other nations on how a private television network can make the democratic process more accessible. In the late '70s Congress, too, was a model of openness in first making the decision to televise its sessions. Since then, other national legislatures—Great Britain, Japan, Germany and Turkey, to name a few—have gone on TV, many of them allowing complete journalistic access.

That's why we believe it's time for Congress to finish the job it began in 1979. It should fully open its debates to television media cameras. And it is our hope that Congress will eventually repeal the must-carry provision and safeguard the free media marketplace that first allowed C-SPAN to flourish.

Brian Lamb is chairman and chief executive officer of C-SPAN.

12

Showtime for Democracy

Reuven Frank

Early and quickly, the television tube evolved into the shape of the proscenium arch, probably to accommodate motion pictures. It thus took its place in the history of public performance, going back at least to when Greek actors played on raised platforms before the painted walls of tents.

All television is theater, or at least to the viewer all television is perceived as theater. In a medium in which consumers may not proceed at the time they choose but only at the pace governed by the presenter, a medium in which images appealing to emotions override information presented by the voice to the ear or by spelled-out words to the eye, exposition and explanation never had a chance. The only thing that could compete for attention with pictures of earthquakes and fires, battles and babies, was the clash of personalities, the impact of conflicting opinions—in short, people arguing, preferably live.

So pity the poor congressman, debating the minutiae in the sub-subsections of appropriations bills and competing for press attention with the president. By 1948, when television came to America, the president had already dominated all the news media through history's worst economic depression; through defeat, despair and, ultimately, victory in history's biggest war and, finally, in undisputed leadership of half of the polarized world that war had left behind.

If their vital constitutional task of legislating could not win the attention of the folks back home, there was one stage on which members of Congress, too, could play—with their exits and their entrances and their many parts—congressional oversight hearings. Hearings came long before television, of course, and some still lived in memory, like Teapot Dome, the prewar sessions of Texas Congressman Martin Dies' House Committee on Un-American Activities (which wondered whether Shirley Temple was subject to communist influence) and, during World War II, the Senate's inquiry into peculation by suppliers of military equipment.

Television was not needed to make the chairman of this last committee, a junior senator from a heartland state, into such an exemplar of rural probity and American toughness that President Roosevelt chose him as a running mate for his fourth campaign to replace the embarrassing Henry Wallace. Thus did a congressional hearing bolster the political career of Harry S. Truman. So it was not that television invented the congressional hearing or even was the first to take advantage of its essential theatricality. But television meant that the theater was always open, the audience always receptive, the press always in attendance.

The first big hearing after World War II played only to still photographers and newsreels, but they established forever the value of pictures. The un-American Activities Committee, under Dies' postwar successors, made the "Hollywood Ten" screenwriters writhe before the camera and bestowed upon Alger Hiss, and his hidden films and the pumpkin he hid them in, the immortality of the picture archive. Richard Nixon's presidency, like all of American politics for the next half-century, is a straight-line descent from the newsreels of the Hiss hearings.

The next hearings hero, master of the proceedings that were the hearings equivalent of *Hamlet, War and Peace* and Beethoven's "Ninth" wrapped into one production, could not quite ride his resulting fame to the presidency. But he came close. In May 1950, Estes Kefauver, the junior senator from Tennessee, was named to the chair of a Senate committee to investigate the influence of organized crime in interstate commerce. It took testimony in 14 cities from 800 witnesses and exposed links between organized crime and politics, angering many politicians.

Wherever the Kefauver committee went it was on television, the new medium, the piece of furniture with the smeary black and white pictures on its window. At first, the pictures were film-edited into manageable chunks for the local evening news. As these seized the attention of the few who owned TV sets and of the local press (leading to trials and unseatings of local political bigwigs), TV stations began sending live cameras—a big effort in those days—and showing the proceedings live, while they were going on. Soap operas, recycled "B" movies and even baseball games were displaced. This was for local broadcast only, but newspapers and wire services were drawing national attention to what was going on.

In the spring of 1951, when the hearings—having shaken up the Chicago Democratic machine and set some of its stalwarts on the road to prison—were headed for New York, the networks judged Kefauver's committee to be worth their attention. The New York sessions were carried across the country, actually the half of the country reached by the interconnected network. Not only that, they were sponsored! Televised congressional hearings had arrived.

Wherever they were seen, the Kefauver hearings commanded attention. Work slowed as people gathered before the windows of television stores. The evening radio and television news and the next morning's newspapers repeated lengthy highlights to rapt audiences and readers. Even afternoon newspapers, then still alive and well, strained to come up with a fresh bulletin for each edition.

On a perfect stage—the temporary hearing room in downtown Manhattan—a universal plot was played by a terrific cast. There was Kefauver himself, a corporate lawyer with a degree from Yale before he entered politics, playing the same Tennessee hillbilly role that he had used to win election. His speech pattern was consciously regional, his voice modulated, his tones measured. Rudolph Halley, the chief counsel, was the kid in the tortoiseshell glasses who always went to the head of the class. He chivvied and worried a parade of officials and mobsters with equal lack of deference. New Hampshire's Republican Sen. Charles Tobey was the New England Yankee from Central Casting, cutting through cant and dissimulation with nuggets of harsh truth: "You were the bagman, weren't you?"

And the witnesses. Oh, the witnesses! The slick, beefy U.S. ambassador to Mexico admitting that while mayor of New York he had taken campaign money from questionable people and might even have helped some of their friends find city jobs. The Anastasia brothers, Albert and Anthony, one a known gangster, the other a "figure" in the famously crooked longshoremen's union, describing their fraternal get-togethers: "Tony, how's the wife and famil'?" Virginia Hill, showgirl turned mobster's moll, not quite as stunning as when she was mistress of the late Bugsy Siegel, described her role as courier for gangland cash.

And Frank Costello, the biggest mobster of them all, he of the puffy face and tiny eyes, the pearl-gray fedora and the voice like cement mixing, the constant cigarettes and the twitchy hands. After he objected to having his face on camera while he testified, all we saw were those hands—clasped and clenched, his fingers drumming, his nails scratching. At the time there was not a better show on television, and there have been few as good since. What they did for crime control in the United States, other than introduce the country to the Fifth Amendment to the Constitution, is not clear. But at a time when only one in five American homes boasted sets, it did wonders for television.

And it changed politics. The public saw Kefauver as the crusader, the good guy humbling the bad guys. Television followed him, because he was Kefauver, to its first New Hampshire primary, where he did so well that President Harry Truman decided not to seek re-election. Kefauver won all but three of the Democratic Party's 1952 presidential primaries. Unfortunately for him, primaries did not yet choose presidential candidates. The city machines, outraged at how Kefauver had exposed their shady connections and sent their loyalists to prison, humbled him at the convention and nominated Illinois Gov. Adlai Stevenson, who in turn lost to Gen. Dwight D. Eisenhower.

The committee's chief counsel, Rudolph Halley, was an unknown lawyer until the televised hearings made him a star. Now all but forgotten but then one of the biggest names in the news, Halley parlayed his fame into winning the presidency of the New York City Council.

Congressional hearings meant not only venue and plot and cast, they also could make stars. And there were always new stars waiting. The now-Republican Senate gave Wisconsin's junior senator an investigating committee chairmanship and the McCarthy era arrived. The stage was the same but as for the plot, both the McCarthy and Kefauver hearings had more in common than we liked to think at the time. In both, witnesses helpless before committee subpoenas were held up to the pillorying gaze of the television camera. The distinction between suspected hoodlums and hapless clerks suspected of leftist thoughts diminishes when the lights go on and the Bill of Rights is mangled.

In sporadic bursts of public sessions, some carried on live television, some only in edited clips in newscasts, McCarthy and his counsel, Roy Cohn, became stars. (Cohn's mother would telephone my boss, NBC News President Bill McAndrew, during hearings to ask if Roy would be on television that evening.) Most of the victims were small fry; the bigger names brought down by "the McCarthy era" fell mostly to other forces, such as the White House's loyalty apparatus, the State Department's fear and cowardice, and the House un-American Activities Committee now chaired by J. Parnell Thomas. But only McCarthy, and to a lesser degree Cohn, achieved lasting stardom.

Then they went too far. Searching for communists in the military, they found a dentist with suspected leftist affiliations who had been routinely promoted from captain to major. When the Pentagon refused to surrender whoever allowed the promotion, McCarthy turned on the Army, humiliating Secretary Robert T. Stevens in an open, televised hearing. (He was also reported outraged by the Army's refusal to grant a draft deferment to a young assistant of Cohn's.) The Senate rounded on its obstreperous member, and McCarthy was himself subjected to Senate investigation. Whatever stardom he had achieved before was as nothing to what he then attained. He advanced from Helen Hayes to Sarah Bernhardt.

Once again, the nation was transfixed. McCarthy in his obstructionism made "Point of Order" part of the language. And, as so often happens on the stage, he made a star of the player playing against him, the special committees counsel Joseph Welch, whose eloquence shamed the senator before the world as a bully and a sneak. McCarthy's career soon ended. Welch returned to private practice. Both are now dead. Both are now immortal. McCarthyism has entered the language as a pejorative term for those on the right as well as those on the left.

After that, Sen. John McClellan of Arkansas tried to stage a revival of Kefauver's scenario about organized crime. Even the lowliest cutpurse knew his Fifth Amendment rights by then, and it was one of McClellan's favorite routines to express wonder and horror that a witness before the Senate would fear that even reciting his name and address would tend to incriminate him. Then, in 1966, Arkansas' other senator, J. William Fulbright, the Senate's foremost opponent of American involvement in Vietnam, had his Foreign Relations Committee examine the conduct of the war. Secretary of State Dean Rusk was the first witness.

Live cameras did not come, only film, as for any important committee where open hearings might—or might not—mean open disagreement. What they recorded, what was shown on the networks' evening news broadcasts that night, was the worst savaging in living memory of a cabinet officer by a senator. Fulbright was withering in his denunciation; Rusk shriveled before the onslaught. The drama was in the conflict of the two aging men representing the two sides of the debate that was splitting America at the time—support for the Vietnam War and opposition to it. Also, it played well on television.

Live cameras were sent the next day, but they were too late. The drama was over. George F. Kennan, foreign-policy establishmentarian and academic guru, was one of several offering a measured, scholarly appraisal of the mistakes of Vietnam involvement. The incident is remembered, if at all, because CBS, the most profitable of the networks during the daytime, chose not to carry the hearings, which led Fred Friendly, seeing Kennan on ABC and NBC while CBS showed yet another rerun of "I Love Lucy," to resign as president of CBS News. That drama was not shown live on television.

The year 1971 brought the Watergate break-in, 1974 the resignation of a president. Most histories of those years deal with the courts and the law officers, Sirica, Jaworski, Elliot Richardson, Archibald Cox. But those who remember those days remember television. They remember the Senate and House hearings; the two judiciary committee chairmen, magisterial Sam Ervin and agonized Peter Rodino; the biblical wrath of Barbara Jordan; some of the witnesses; and, above all, the event itself—the history and the tragedy, the survival of "the system." This, too, was unforgettable theater, exalted by its subject to Wagnerian opera.

After that, there seems little worth remembering. Iran-Contra held center stage for its hour or two and went its way. By the time of the hearings it was already before the courts, and the Democratic chairman and his counsel were inhibited. They may also have sensed that the nation was not in the mood for another Watergate and laid themselves open to outrageous manipulation by Oliver North, by his brilliant counsel and by the wire pullers back in the Reagan White House.

Now such hearings as there are show up on C-SPAN and CNN while the rest of television, the networks and stations and cable channels, go about their uninterrupted business. The existence of C-SPAN relieves the networks of what they used to see as their moral responsibility, to transmit important news at whatever discomfort. Why bother? Those who want it can see it on C-SPAN.

Occasionally, there are unexpected explosions and there will probably be more. The sudden prominence of Anita Hill in the confirmation hearings for Clarence Thomas' nomination to the Supreme Court became a major television event because they exposed so many raw nerves of the country that year, that month, that day.

Whitewater and Waco cause occasional small flurries, but only public television joined cable in carrying the earlier proceedings, and then rarely. The novelty that had enraptured citizens watching the Kefauver hearings in appliance store windows is long past. The element of the morality play, of Good triumphing over Evil, seems gone. Perhaps the public's much discussed current cynicism leads viewers to distrust the accusers as much as the accused. Also, after the O.J. Simpson trial, what can a congressional hearing offer? The public is always at its most fickle when seeking entertainment.

As people say about Broadway, these are not good years for congressional hearings. Or perhaps, as other people say about Broadway, the great days are over. Thus closes another channel between the members of Congress and the voter.

Reuven Frank, a 1988–89 Media Studies Center senior fellow, was twice president of NBC News. He is author of Out of Thin Air *and writes a regular column for* The New Leader.

13

Hollywood Goes to Congress

Tom Rosenstiel

Imagine a U.S. senator of limited wisdom, a few bad habits and one especially foolish idea: he keeps a diary. The senator thinks it will make interesting reading: he's a member of the Senate, after all, the nation's most august deliberative body. And just in case he gets in trouble with his colleagues, the thing would make great blackmail. So each day, he writes down everything—sex and corruption and political shenanigans, all the Senate's secrets. Eventually, of course, the diary falls into the hands of his enemies. He fights to keep his seat anyway—he has no other skills in life other than being a blustering pol—but in the end he resigns in disgrace.

It sound like a good script, a chronicle of The Bob Packwood Story. Actually, Hollywood already produced this tale nearly 50 years ago, in a forgotten gem of 1948 called *The Senator Was Indiscreet*. The film, a sophisticated farce, offers a helpful caution when we think about politics: in this age when we decry the public's distrust of institutions and loss of faith in leaders, it is worthwhile to remember that cynicism about Congress is an old story.

Consider these five films made over five decades: *Mr. Smith Goes to Washington* (1939), *The Senator Was Indiscreet* (1948), *Advise and Consent* (1962), *The Seduction of Joe Tynan* (1979) and *Distinguished Gentleman* (1992). All enjoyed some critical acclaim and financial success; all cover similar subjects and themes.

Taken together, they reveal several surprises about how America has viewed Congress for much of the century. The popular image of the place, although biting and angry from the start, has actually improved with time. The most reverent images of our legislative process did not come during the New Deal or World War II but in the 1960s (during the Kennedy era) and in the 1970s (after Watergate). And rather than becoming more sophisticated, the popular image of our legislature has gradually become more one dimensional.

Throughout these films, however, a few themes are constant. Politicians are often depicted as decent and well-meaning folks led astray by the system, by avarice, by power or by evil political brokers (usually businessmen). We may imagine cynical PR handlers to be recent inventions, but they have always been part of congressional mythology. And the imagery of the press has never been good. Actually, it's gone from bad (smart but jaded opportunists) to better (earnest but jaded opportunists) to bland (powerful and manipulable opportunists).

The first major movie about Congress, and arguably the best, is Frank Capra's *Mr. Smith Goes to Washington.* The movie is the story of Jefferson Smith (James Stewart), a politically naive Boy Scout leader who is named to fill a two-month vacancy in the Senate and finds mostly corruption and greed. Jim Taylor, a newspaper publisher and business magnate who runs Smith's home state, has masterminded a plot to buy up land through dummy corporations and then have the federal government buy it from him at inflated prices to build a dam. Smith unwittingly runs afoul of Taylor when he proposes building a summer camp for boys on the same land. Taylor smears Smith, but the young senator stands up to the bosses and eventually shames the Senate into yielding.

People usually recall *Mr. Smith* as a celebration of naive idealism, another example of Hollywood coping with the Depression by making fantasy and myth. But like most Capra films, it is wry stuff below the surface, full of sadness and worldliness. The film endures not because Jimmy Stewart is so swell, but because it depicts the subtle and credible humanity of the hack reporters, the bad senator, the overly partisan opposition leader and the taciturn vice president.

When cynical reporters make a fool of Smith (they get him to pose holding his nose and then write captions about how he thinks the Senate stinks), the young senator is so outraged he punches them out. But Capra sympathizes with the jaded reporters. "You're not a senator, you're an honorary stooge. You ought to be shown up," one tells Smith. Grudgingly, Smith agrees. The governor who appoints Smith, a Taylor machine stooge, is depicted with a sympathetic irony. The governor, named "Happy," is congenitally depressed by Taylor's calling the shots.

Even Joseph Paine, the corrupt senator who sponsored the dam to enrich Taylor, is a tragic and sympathetic figure, as played by Claude Rains, the actor who made a career of walking the line between good and evil with characters like Louis, the police chief in *Casablanca*. Once a crusading lawyer, Paine tries on several occasions to walk away from the political boss but can't. When he admits the dam project to Smith, his explanation is close to winning: "I compromised so that all these years I could sit in that Senate and serve the people in a thousand honest ways. But I've had to compromise. I've had to play ball. You can't count on people voting. Half the time they don't vote anyway. That's how states and empires have been built since time began."

Released in 1939, *Mr. Smith* was made for a politically uncertain America. Franklin Roosevelt's New Deal was losing popularity. The Depression dragged on. Much of the film is about doubting. Capra, for instance, has a sophisticated vision of how public opinion is "Taylor made," as one reporter puts it. When political boss Taylor wants to generate support for Smith's Senate appointment, he tells his political lieutenant to stage what sounds like a modern TV photo-op. "Turn the ballyhoo boys loose," he says.

Capra even has some distance from his hero, Jeff Smith. At one point he is described as "a squirrel chaser, a simpleton of all times, a big-eyed patriot," and he is. Smith finally prevails only because more cunning people are moved by his simple goodness and come to his aid to school him in the subtleties of Senate rules or, like the vice president who presides over the Senate, to subtly exercise parliamentary discretion to protect him.

Capra's Senate is corrupt and honorable, filled with men of intellect and instinct who compromise too much but know a decent thing when they see it. Politics is not a dirty word, it's just vulnerable to abuse by a minority of dishonest men who "just throw big shadows," as one character says. The film is not a cartoon about the power of goodness but an appeal for people to aim high and not compromise too easily. "Lincoln had his Taylors" the savvy Senate aide (Jean Arthur) tells Smith as he prepares to give up. "So did every other man who ever tried to lift his thoughts up off the ground. Odds against them didn't stop those men.

They were fools that way. All the good that ever came into this world came from fools with faith like that."

Nine years later, major Hollywood talents turned to Congress again. *The Senator Was Indiscreet* is not really more jaded about political manipulation than *Mr. Smith*, but it describes a political world filled by hacks and phonies rather than bright but misled men. The main character is diary-writing Sen. Melvin G. Ashton, a pompous nincompoop who wants to be president. Ashton's political talents, as they are conjured up by writer Charles MacArthur (co-author of *The Front Page*) and director George S. Kaufman (the Broadway satirist), are a deep baritone voice, a silvery mane and absurd ambition. Ashton comes to a New York hotel to begin his campaign for president. The party thinks he is too stupid to run, but Ashton threatens to release his diary if they try to stop him. His candidacy takes off, thanks to his shrewd PR man, until he loses his diary. In the end, the diary becomes public, and Ashton and the party hacks flee to an obscure Pacific island, the only place where they are unknown.

People complain that television has turned politics into something phony, but in this film congressional politics is all stage management. Ashton's campaign is a blur of inanities. His platform planks are "Against Inflation" and "Against Depression." He climbs in the polls after posing with beauty queens in bathing suits like "Miss Tomato Juice." When the party boss complains about Ashton's presidential ambitions, the senator's PR man defends the candidate's credibility with this inspiring thought: "If you can sell the American public the idea that one cigarette is different from another or that one toothpaste is better than another, you can sell them anything. Even Mel Ashton."

Reporters are in on the game, protecting the boobs who control political power. The PR man even becomes incensed when a reporter threatens to quote Ashton verbatim. "You can't go around quoting politicians accurately. That's dirty journalism and you know it." Elements of this farce hit subtly home to the modern ear. The purpose of Ashton's campaign swing is not about issues but about making the senator likable. "We have to show the public you're a human being," his PR man explains.

Indiscreet is harmless stuff—it's biting but it doesn't break the skin. The film dismisses politics: Congress is run by bumpkins and blowhards, but it doesn't much matter in people's lives. There is none of the modern sense of dependence on government to solve problems.

That changed 14 years later, after the Cuban Missile Crisis and Sputnik. In political films of the early 1960s, we see a new element of respectfulness about the people in government, especially the loyal veterans who populate Congress. This respect for the process and institutions and men of Congress reaches its height in *Advise and Consent,* based on Allen Drury's novel, directed by Otto Preminger and released in 1962. The film portrays the Senate as it grapples with a controversial appointment for secretary of state. The president has appointed a liberal intellectual to the post, Robert Leffingwell, played by Henry Fonda. Conservatives want to stop him for being too soft on communism. So does a shrewd Southern Democrat, Seabright Cooley, played by Charles Laughton. At the confirmation hearings, Cooley unearths a fragile federal clerk who charges that he was once part of a communist cell with Leffingwell at the University of Chicago. Leffingwell destroys his accuser, but the truth is more subtle. He did flirt with communism—and then rejected it. But in the political climate of the Cold War there is no room for subtlety. As senators begin to find out that Leffingwell lied, powers on both sides resort to dastardly methods to manipulate the vote—including blackmail—until one senator, threatened with exposure for a homosexual fling in the Navy, commits suicide.

For all the soap-opera dramatics, Preminger's *Advise and Consent* celebrates the subtle, cold pragmatism of the Kennedy age. Its extols the political establishment, the Congress and even the senators, with their irony and bombast. Reporters are portrayed as faceless pencil pushers ready to exploit any conflict. The film's hero, however, is not Leffingwell, the Adlai Stevenson-type intellectual who is wronged for having flirted with communism. Ultimately, Preminger sees Leffingwell as a bit too distant and superior, and too impractical.

Preminger's hero in the film is the unflappable Senate Majority Leader Bob Munson, played by the stately Walter Pidgeon as a wise and worldly survivor, a protector of the Congress as an institution. He stoically fights for Leffingwell's confirmation, even though he would have preferred a more popular choice, because that is his job as leader—to serve his party and his president—and because he believes in personal loyalty. When the president dies in the final moments of the film and the vice president proposes to withdraw the Leffingwell nomination and pick someone else, the majority leader promises he will do everything he can to see that the new man is confirmed, whoever he is.

Preminger's choice of bad guy is also revealing. It's not Cooley, the treacherous Southern Democrat who wants to destroy the Leffingwell nomination. Cooley is old-fashioned and a little endearing. Unaffected by the trappings of power, he rides the streetcar to work. In private, Cooley and his public adversary the majority leader are friendly poker partners. In the final scene, when they both decide to release their votes and let people vote their consciences, they delight in the drama of the moment. After Cooley agrees not to stand in Leffingwell's way, the majority leader even praises him and faintly denounces Leffingwell. "I hope the day never comes when there is not at least one curmudgeon in this body to goad us in the right direction," he says. The film admires the subtle and complex dimensions of Congress—the friendships between political enemies, men who lead with their minds rather than their emotions—and the majority leader embodies all of these.

The villain in *Advise and Consent* is the hotheaded liberal senator who tries to use blackmail to get Leffingwell into office on the grounds that the country really needs him. "We tolerate just about anything here," the majority leader tells the young liberal. "Prejudice, avarice, demagoguery. That's what the Senate's for, to tolerate freedom." But it can't abide blackmail. Ultimately, the liberal extremist is driven from the Senate; his departure costs Leffingwell his confirmation, but the majority leader doesn't care. The integrity of the Senate is more important than Leffingwell. Ideological extremism, Preminger argues, is worse than cynicism. Newt Gingrich and the new GOP would be the bad guys in this film. Bob Dole and Bob Byrd, moderates of either party, the old-fashioned legislators whose word is their bond, would be the heroes.

Next to extremism, the other danger, according to Hollywood, is too much idealism. The majority leader grants the honor of chairing the Leffingwell hearings to Sen. Briggs Anderson of Utah because he is a moderate. But Anderson in the end is too much of a Boy Scout. He is unduly offended by Leffingwell's lies, for instance, and unable to appreciate the irony of Leffingwell's predicament. Ultimately it does him in. When Anderson decides to vote against Leffingwell on moral grounds, and then is blackmailed by Leffingwell backers, he commits suicide.

The world, Preminger is arguing, is much more complicated than a simple struggle between good and evil. Seventeen years later, in the aftermath of Watergate, a good deal of this pragmatism survives in *The Seduction of Joe Tynan,* a character study about congressional power, starring Alan Alda, who also wrote the screenplay. Ostensibly, Tynan is a cautionary tale about what happens to a decent senator when he begins to become a national figure. He is seduced, literally, by a young civil rights lawyer from Louisiana who is excited by the possibility of being a president's mistress. But the real seduction is power. The film traces Tynan as he leads the opposition to the Supreme Court nomination of a Louisiana judge on behalf of civil rights groups. Tynan knows that while the man is no saint, he is not really a racist. But Tynan also knows that leading the charge will propel him into a possible presidential bid.

For all its musing about power, however, Tynan does not view Congress as corrupt. In the view of this film, politics is important enough work, done by able men. Too bad it has to be so cynical, but ultimately the system works. Just keep a little distance, if you can. Tynan's sins are forgiven in the end because underneath his compromises he's such a decent guy. The press, which senses that Tynan is beginning to make compromises, is deflected by Tynan's charm. Even Tynan's wife, whom he has neglected, cheated on and all but left to raise two warring kids, forgives him. In the final scene, at a national convention where the crowd is in love with Tynan, she silently nods that she will stay with him, even though she knows he is about to be lost to an adoring public. His country, presumably, needs him. In its moral ennui, the film is a kind of apologia to people like Ted Kennedy or even Bob Packwood, whose private failures are forgiven because they make good laws.

What is most alarming, perhaps, is the chasm one feels only 13 years later in the latest film about Congress, *Distinguished Gentleman*. The sophisticated hymn to faith that we saw in *Mr. Smith,* the mocking but gentle ribbing of *The Senator Was Indiscreet* and the subtle celebration of the process of the 1960s and even the 1970s are gone. *Distinguished Gentleman* is not forgiving; it depicts a Washington where little seems worth caring about.

Released in 1992, *Gentleman* is the story of Thomas Jefferson Jones, a small-time Florida con man (Eddie Murphy), who becomes convinced that Washington is the biggest con game of all. When his local congressman (James Garner) has a heart attack and dies en flagrante delicto with his secretary, Jones, who has the same middle and last name as the dead congressman, decides to run in his place. (His slogan "Jeff Jones: The Name You Know.") Since voters are too ignorant to know the difference, he wins. Jones' crooked skills serve him well in D.C., until he falls in love with a young environmentalist and decides to expose a corrupt committee chairman and the evil power companies he's protecting.

The corruption in *Distinguished Gentleman* is not about ideology (as it is in *Advise and Consent*) or about power (as in Joe Tynan and The Senator was Indiscreet). It is all about money. After he arrives in Washington, a lobbyist advises Jones on which committees are best for extorting funds from special interests. When the lobbyist asks Jones where he stands on sugar price supports, and Jones wonders which is better, he hears this:

"Shit makes no difference to me," the lobbyist says. "If you're for 'em, I've got money from sugar producers. If you're against, I've got money from candy manufacturers."

Jones asks, "Terry, tell me, with all this money coming in from both sides, how can anything ever possibly get done?"

"It doesn't," says the lobbyist. "That's the genius of the system."

By 1992, it isn't bad people who are to blame. The whole system is rigged, voters are idiots and campaign rhetoric is laughable. The portrayal of the press in this film marks a distinct departure. The jaded but savvy reporters have given way to a herd of cameras and microphones that are there to be manipulated by whichever side can provide them with the most compelling tape.

Jones delivers one memorable campaign speech, the night of his victory: "We ran a positive campaign. We campaigned on the issues. The issue is change. Change for the future. The people have spoken. Live free or die. And in conclusion, read my lips."

In the end, even Jones doesn't change anything. He just runs a couple of bad guys out of town by capturing their corruption on videotape. He doesn't even remind people of their goodness, like Jeff Smith did 55 years before. Jones is just another con man. In the final scene his idealistic girlfriend asks him what he will do next. "I've got a full head of hair, a famous face and pretty good bullshit," he says. "There's only one thing I can do. I'm going to run for president."

The film is pure anger against a system that seems unredeemable. Is it any wonder that the year this film was released the public booted out an incumbent president, George Bush, or that two years later it booted out the party that had run Congress for 40 years, and that 11 months after that, the public is losing faith again with the Republicans it just put in charge?

These five films trace an arc, from hope in *Mr. Smith* to madcap fun in *The Senator Was Indiscreet* to a sense of renewed expectations about government in Advise and Consent to simple disgust and antipathy in *Distinguished Gentleman*. Neither cynicism about Congress nor anger about corruption is new. What is new is utter hopelessness. One cannot help but have some sympathy for whoever tries to raise expectations again. Unless they can change politics into something other than what it appears to be in these films, the public will be hard to satisfy.

Tom Rosenstiel, a former congressional correspondent for Newsweek's *Washington bureau and the author of* Strange Bedfellows: How Television and the Presidential Candidates Changed American Politics, 1992, *is director of the Pew Charitable Trust's Project for Excellence in Journalism.*

14

Coverage—The Void at Home

Martin Weinberger

The scene is repeated frequently these days: Newt Gingrich, speaker of the House of Representatives, stands before a patch of microphones as plentiful as cornstalks in an Iowa field. The speaker has become the property of the nation, the recipient of the contemporary cult of personality. His commentary on political deliberations easily makes news.

Ironically, as all this transpires, the other 434 members of the House of Representatives labor in relative anonymity—even in their own districts. Judging from sampling a number of California's 106 daily and 315 weekly newspapers, the activities of an individual member of Congress are reported either superficially or not at all. And in this case, it seems that as California goes, so goes the nation.

The weaknesses of congressional coverage are apparent in both large and small newspapers. In large metropolitan or chain newspapers with Washington bureaus, the area of circulation often is too large to focus on an individual member. Coverage will most likely consist of a wide-ranging survey of multiple congressional districts, with an emphasis on nefarious behavior. Smaller dailies and weeklies, which in theory are better positioned to cover an individual representative, too often deliver reporting that is insubstantial. Either way, readers are left adrift, ignorant of what their representatives are doing.

Why? We live in a period of anti-government sentiment, and newspapers are not known to rise above their readers' preferences. Publishers and editors lament that they ought to do more congressional coverage, but they presume that their readers are not interested in congressional politics and thus report little of it. Even when there is a desire to devote more attention to Congress, the rising cost of newsprint parlays itself into smaller newsholes. And the constant campaign to control costs reduces staff, weakens the opportunity to develop expertise on congressional matters and slices into opportunities for reporting.

A survey of the editors and/or publishers of 41 California newspapers, both dailies and weeklies, reveals four principal forms of congressional coverage: features on particular legislation without any special attention to local representatives; brief summaries of timely legislative action accompanied by the local representative's votes; reprints of the local representative's handouts; and, most often, nothing at all.

Yet the void in newspaper coverage of Congress creates an opportunity for the attentive legislator. Through press releases, staff work, video material, district pork, local office contacts, subsidized mailings, awards and honors to residents and capital visits by constituents, members of Congress can use newspapers to color the quality and depth of their work and to help fend off any challenges to re-election.

"Successful press management leaves newspapers at the mercy of congressmen," says David Menefee-Libey, associate professor of politics at Pomona College. Newspapers that do take a continuing interest in reporting on an individual representative often concentrate on legislative outcomes instead of legislative development. Readers may learn whether or not a bill passes, but they will learn very little, if anything, about how it took shape.

Consider the case of Rep. David Dreier, a conservative Republican in the suburban-turning-urban 28th Congressional District, which stretches along the picturesque (when they are visible through the smog) San Gabriel Mountains of southern California. Five daily and a dozen weekly newspapers circulate in his district. Only one weekly does not endorse him for re-election. Dreier makes use of the advantages accorded to incumbents. He also pays close attention to the newspapers and their reporting. His news releases chronicle the visits and accomplishments of constituents as well as routine items such as applications for the military academies and the awarding of flags that have flown over the Capitol. He visits the newspapers regularly during recesses and engages in discussions with editorial staff representatives, offering additional support for his views. He prepares videotapes in the congressional studio for cable television stations. He sends out franked mailing pieces as permitted by current law, and he solicits editorial endorsements. He will not engage an opponent in the traditional definition of a debate but participates in a limited number of joint appearances during election campaigns with fixed time limits and no cross-questioning, thereby limiting newspaper coverage. In short, Dreier presents a skilled example of how self-interest and manipulation of information can merge.

Journalists who wish to improve on this situation can, however, find newspapers worth emulating. Indeed, enterprising newspapers can present congressional coverage even though they may lack a Washington bureau. The *Riverside (Calif.) Press-Enterprise* (circulation 176,958) has eliminated its bureau in Washington but uses a multitude of means to cover the activities of two local representatives. Marcia McQuern, publisher of the newspaper—now the second-largest family-owned daily in the state—takes her "First Amendment responsibility" seriously. Her own background, first as a political science major in college and then as a reporter in Sacramento, the state capital, has helped shape her interests and turned her into a self-described "political junkie."

The *Press-Enterprise* publishes weekly voting records with an emphasis on important issues. A wrap-up of issues at the end of a congressional session is developed using wire services and Washington free-lancers to help develop the story. Readers are informed frequently on how to write to a member of Congress.

Additional feature material is offered to create a clear view of a congressman's activities—for example, a story developed around Congressman Sonny Bono's, R-Calif., first year in office. Congressional candidates are interviewed at election time in order to make endorsements. The newspaper seeks to maintain a "professional relationship" in connection with such interviews; both of the endorsed candidates failed to win election in 1994, yet the successful representatives have continued to maintain contact with the *Press-Enterprise*—despite the newspaper's rejecting for publication most of the material sent from the congressional offices.

The situation grows murkier among smaller publications. California community newspapers that win many honors and awards for their journalism garner their acclaim despite the fact that they present no week-by-week reporting of congressional votes or issues. Nevertheless, there are some sustained efforts at coverage in the weeklies.

William Johnson, a former congressional aide and now publisher of the *Palo Alto (Calif.) Weekly* (circulation 50,500) places interest-group ratings above the publication of voting records. He sees dangers in brief summaries of legislation when viewed against the arcane substance of the laws. The *Weekly* editorial policy is to offer background information dealing with a specific issue or legislator while it skips regular reports on votes or interest group reactions.

Ideally, at the minimum, a newspaper covering Congress and its members presents a listing of the representative's votes along with a summary of issues. Issues that are particularly sensitive to the community should be explored. For example: a town with an older readership needs local views on the consequences of changes in Medicare, a subject most often discussed in terms of billions of dollars without establishing particular meaning for the individual.

Reporters usually wait for a schedule of personal appearances to emanate from the representative's office. Instead, they should be more aggressive in setting up interviews because face-to-face questioning can produce insight into issues.

And a newspaper's endorsement at election time should be based on who ought to be elected, not who will be elected. The temptation is great to add to a newspaper's reputation by selecting the winner. That sort of selection makes a mockery of the newspaper's proper function and its obligation to readers.

Extensive resources exist at nominal cost to provide a newspaper reporter with the specifics of congressional action. A half century ago, Nelson Poynter, a St. Petersburg, Fla., publisher, began the Congressional Quarterly service from Washington to meet the information needs of journalists covering the federal government. A branch of that operation, the *Weekly Report,* now serves 267 newspapers, most of them daily, and 39 broadcasters throughout the country. It offers a comprehensive description of voting records, the content of bills, committee activities and related topics. While straightening out the zigzagging lines of legislation, its coverage tends to be "official," omitting the human drama enveloping political behavior.

Another source of information is the ever-growing World Wide Web and on-line information services. These offer the journalist not only immediate coverage but also extensive background information.

Journalists looking for more information on Congress can also turn to Project Vote Smart, an offshoot of the Center for National Independence in Politics. Project Vote Smart, established with former Presidents Jimmy Carter and Gerald Ford as honorary co-founders, offers access to information that helps fill the growing hole in local political reporting. Richard Kimball, the project's board president and a former Arizona state legislator, recalls that when the program began in 1992, its offices in Corvallis, Ore., were swamped with requests for information. A separate system for journalists from newspapers, radio and television has since been established, offering issue reviews by region, resource materials, congressional snapshots and key votes.

With cutbacks in political reporting throughout the nation and more space being moved from governmental coverage to graphics and photography, "reporters are [operating] under stress," Kimball says. Political reporting might be only one minor portion of a burdened journalist's tasks, leading to such questions as, "Where is the electoral college located?"

Project Vote Smart publishes ratings of members of the House and Senate as developed by 17 interest groups. Although the net result is an insightful description of an individual's governmental philosophy, few newspapers publish them. Kimball's experience underscores the need for immediate and easy access to material about Congress.

Although politicians and political behavior are currently held in low esteem, the process of government reaches into areas of high drama as well as plain nonsense. What do representatives or senators do with their time? Do they have influence among their colleagues? What is happening in committee that affects the newspaper's readers? How does a representative participate in the give-and-take of developing legislation? What are a representative's sources of information? The shirtsleeve workings of the political process form the bedrock of democratic self-government, but unfortunately they remain buried in the cloakroom.

Congress offers a continuous foray into the very nature of power. The newspaper—large and small, daily and weekly—bears an obligation to report how and by whom that power is used. Unfortunately, most newspapers seem to hear that obligation in the form of a whisper rather than a clarion call.

Martin Weinberger is publisher and editor in chief of the Claremont (Calif.) Courier.

15

Kingmakers, Kingbreakers

Shirley Williams

I am, I suppose, an outsider in the United States. I lecture at Harvard's John F. Kennedy School of Government, but I am more a politician than an academic, having spent nearly 20 years of my life in the British Parliament. I lecture on, among other things, American politics. For the past seven years as a professor here, and on numerous visits lasting from months to years since I was a child, I have observed and wondered at the complexities, idiosyncrasies and individualism of American politics.

I have watched the decline of the Democratic Party in Congress, the result of fragmentation, indiscipline and a lack of agreed objectives. I have watched the renaissance of the Republicans and their brilliant planning over many years to recruit and commit legislators at local, state and federal levels. I have felt a growing concern that American democracy, once the envy of free men and women everywhere, is being devoured by money as ivy devours oak trees. And I have observed the increasing stature of the U.S. media, which has moved from commenting on kings to making and breaking them.

Coverage of Congress in the serious American newspapers is much fuller than I would see of the House of Commons in Britain for the very good reason that Congress is much more important. Nowadays, except when majorities are fragile, as is John Major's, or when parties split, the executive has effectively tamed the House of Commons by patronage, party discipline and occasional threats.

Because the outcomes of votes are largely predictable, and because the public prefers sitcoms and dramas to politics, coverage of Parliament has been very much curtailed. Regular pages of the print press dedicated to Parliament have been switched to other topics. After parliamentary questions, and perhaps two front-bench speeches if there is a major controversial debate, the press galleries are empty. However eloquent their remarks, no budding Disraeli or Gladstone—speaking, as freshmen do, late in a debate—is likely to be reported.

There are many things the British print media can learn from the United States. British print journalists more often write as if they are ideologically committed than do their American counterparts. You don't have to be very bright to discover that the *Daily Telegraph* supports the conservatives and that The *Guardian* supports the Liberal Democrats and the Labor Party. The *New York Times* has a liberal bias and people like Sen. Phil Gramm, R-Texas, will tell us so, but it is less obvious than partisanship in the British press.

Second, American journalists show less deference towards their bosses. In Britain, media proprietors have a lot of influence over content, whatever they may say.

Then there is the sheer seriousness of American political reporting—the detail, the long quotations from key players, the careful analysis. If I really want to know what happened, the *Los Angeles Times,* the *New York Times* or the *Washington Post* will give me much more comprehensive coverage than even the best British newspaper.

There is, however, one big qualification, and it is an important one. Serious American newspapers seem to revisit certain subjects over and over, while neglecting others. I can find little about South Asia or Africa here, and coverage of the European Union or Latin America is sporadic. To keep up with international happenings other than world headline events, I need the *Financial Times* daily and, in addition, *The Economist.*

My favorable comparisons of the print press do not extend to television, partly because there are few late-night political programs. Outside of C-SPAN, television coverage of Congress tends to be quite superficial and concentrates on a handful of leading figures, mainly in a news format. Dramatic events and personalities are the stuff of television, with little attention given to deliberation. It is, of course, pointed out that there isn't much of an audience for political programs, and that the audience there consists of addicts so hooked on politics that they watch not one but several political programs weekly. The estimated

16.7 million people (according to Mediamark Research) who watch C-SPAN at some time in the week may come close to the limit of potential viewers. But good coverage of issues affecting men and women far beyond the Beltway might augment the number.

In Britain, the BBC influences, and has been influenced by, commercial television. The regulators there seem to be tougher in insisting on a proportion of current affairs programs in television listings, and ratings are not the sole—or practically sole—criterion for allocating time or approving license bids. There are long documentary programs like "Panorama" every week, as well as those with a question or discussion format, like "Question Time" (weekly), "Newsnight" (nightly) and the radio program "Any Questions." These programs allow long periods of time, anything from five to 20 minutes, for exploration of an issue without the constant interruptions of commercials. Furthermore, much of the questioning is directly by the public, not mediated by journalists. Journalists themselves are as often on the panel answering as in the audience interrogating.

The tone of American congressional coverage is what one might call superior skepticism. The skepticism is the product of congressional self-laceration: surely nowhere else do legislators run so consistently and passionately against their own institution. It is also a product of the damage done to Congress by a series of financial and sexual scandals. These factors have contributed greatly to a media presentation that in turn feeds public cynicism and disgust.

The superior note comes from the media's self-perception as watchdog, scourge and purifier. Since Watergate, some media stars have seen themselves as kingmakers and kingbreakers. It is a tempting and perilous role. Certainly the media play a vital part in American government. They are the transmitters and channels between the different parts of this disparate and separated structure, its nervous system. But they are not themselves either the government or the sovereign people.

Polls, conducted by news networks and presented as news events, have allowed the media to arrogate to themselves the role of the people's voice. Investigative journalism has substituted for congressional inquiry. The media, in a democratic society, are indispensable but should not feel they can themselves dispense with other institutions (including elections), nor regard the First Amendment as absolving them from responsibility for the public good. The outcry about the Energy Department's rather crude attempt to rate journalists covering the Department shows how sensitive the media are to the very treatment they hand out.

The decline of political parties as institutions of political communication has also shaped the coverage of Congress in recent years. In its long decline from overwhelming power in the House, the Democratic Party has lost any sense of solidarity. (I think of it as rather like the Ottoman Empire after the First World War.) More and more American citizens are not clear on what the outcome of an election actually means in terms of policies and laws. Each representative has his or her own agenda. Politics has become a collection of bargains rather than a competition between clear and cohesive programs.

What House Speaker Newt Gingrich has done (he's not my politics, but the process is impressive) is to rebuild loyalty to certain objectives embraced by the Party leaders. Gingrich and his colleagues, in the House and in the Republican Party, have provided the necessary long-term support, encouragement, training and sometimes funds for bright young men and women coming up through local and state government and appearing 10 years later at the federal level. It has been a brilliantly planned and executed strategy.

My impression is that the new electronic media, such as e-mail and the Internet, have been useful but not essential in the Republican ascent. A large part of the Republican effort relied on some pretty old technologies such as audiotapes and videotapes, especially the former. A senior legislator in a Republican state told me that the brilliance of the Republican media strategy rested on the simple perception that lawmakers spend much time driving from place to place. So the Gingrich team distributed audiotapes for legislators to play while they drove.

I still distinguish, however, between the print media and the others because the print media reflect something of the old tradition of civic education. As I understand it from some of my students, "civic journalism" is now emerging at the local level in an attempt to encourage deliberation on issues and to formulate common interests in social and community cohesion against the fragmenting and disintegrating pressures of special interests. I don't know quite how one captures the idea of social cohesion (in Europe it is known as solidarity), but I do know that it is the coming theme of politics: obligations as well as rights, fellowship, the mutual bonds that bind communities together.

Achieving social cohesion is made more difficult by some of the recent technological advances in communication. Cable television, for instance, enables politicians to speak to closely defined and targeted audiences. So do videos focused on particular groups and interests. So does direct computerized mail.

There are voices raised now suggesting that representative democracy has had its day and should be replaced by direct democracy: local initiatives determined by local referenda, instant telephone polls, electronic home voting. The problems, however, are always the same: How does the instant voter, the instant opinion former, subject his or her views to deliberation, discussion and debate? How does he or she discover the forces manipulating the outcome (money has been found to be the single most important determinant of the outcome of local referenda). Would seasoned and informed opinion that has been subjected to intellectual and empirical tests be the same as when that opinion was first minted?

The evidence from experiments in deliberative television, and indeed in focus groups, suggests that opinions do change, that second thoughts are not identical with first nonthoughts. In its famous production "Granada 500," Granada Television, a big regional independent network in Great Britain, conducted a series of television programs during the course of an election campaign. Each week the same 500 people (carefully chosen to reflect the gender, age, occupational, ethnic and party composition of the electorate) questioned party leaders on a particular issue—crime, taxes and the economy, social issues, foreign affairs—for an hour or more. At the end of the series, voting preferences among the 500 were found to have moved significantly from those registered before the series began.

Town meeting formats in the United States are also promising. We must, however, get away from the idea that measuring spasmodic and instant reactions to words and phrases uttered by a politician is some magic formula for popular democracy.

My greatest worry about the United States is that it is turning inwards at the very time that national economies are going global, and nation-states are trying to evolve some framework of rights and laws capable of civilizing the globalization process. That's an asymmetry that cannot be sustained.

Will the media be able to resist this desire of many Americans to hide, to tell the rest of the world to go to hell? It is not pleasant to be told that our fate, and indeed that of our hard-pressed planet, is in the hands of the international bond markets, and that often those markets know little of what they are doing or why. But I suspect it is the truth. And who have we but the media to bear witness to it?

Shirley Williams is Public Service Professor of Electoral Politics at the John F. Kennedy School of Government, Harvard University, and a member of the British House of Lords. Lady Williams was previously a member of the House of Commons for 17 years and a member of the British Cabinet and a Privy Council.

Part IV

Media and Congress in Historical Perspective

16

Not a Pretty Picture

Joan L. Conners

People looking for positive portrayals of Congress will not find them in political cartoons. Since the 18th century, cartoons have expressed skepticism about the contributions of Congress to American political life and the character of congressional leaders. Cartoonists have rarely portrayed Congress as efficient, effective or ethical; rather, they frequently lampoon it for being confused, contentious and immoral. In short, the Congress that appears in political cartoons is not the ideal embodiment of a democratic institution.

In fairness to our national legislature, it is worth pointing out that this bleak picture is partly the product of the imperatives of the cartoonist's trade. Sarcasm, ridicule and humor are the standard tools of a successful cartoonist. And in a journalistic culture that has long been characterized by the pursuit of objectivity, it has often fallen to the cartoonist to offer the commentary and criticism that are otherwise thwarted by conventional standards of reportorial neutrality.

Yet part of the explanation for the poor image of Congress in the nation's cartoons lies in the nature of the institution itself. Congress, as a legislative body, is powerfully shaped by the arcane processes of lawmaking, by deal making and by the conflicting pressures of local and national interests. All of these provide ample targets for cartoonists. Congress has often been denounced for partisan battles that diminish legislative productivity. Its proceedings are often characterized as inefficient, if not comical. Congressional unity, which might be expected to yield positive portraits, is usually the product of either presidential domination or a congressional challenge to the White House—both of which can easily lead to Congress' appearing in a less-than-flattering posture.

Cartoons also represent a unified Congress as an "old boys' club." Its members, in this vision, are the beneficiaries of unfair privileges, such as self-approved pay raises, and at worst the perpetrators of illegal acts, such as bribery. Twentieth-century cartoons often note Congress' lack of diversity and its obsession with its own narrow interests.

Within these general tendencies, however, it is startling to notice how dramatically caricatures of Congress have evolved—stylistically and conceptually—over the last two centuries. The line drawings of the current era bear little resemblance to the intricate etchings of the 19th century. Throughout the 20th century, but especially in the 1940s and 1950s, renderings became increasingly simplified in message and detail. This can largely be explained by the radical changes in the newspaper industry itself. The demands of daily deadlines and mass circulation meant that production had to be immediate and current, and political cartoons were no exception. Nineteenth-century cartoons generally appeared in elite weeklies, which catered to a smaller, highly educated audience. The mass circulation of 20th-century urban dailies brought to cartoons a larger and more diverse audience, and a new type of commentary and cartooning evolved that would appeal to them. Television, which has made American communication much more visual, also cannot be discounted as an influence on cartoon styles.

In reviewing political cartoons of Congress from the last 200 years, it appears that cartoonists are much more critical of Congress today. While early cartoons represent members of Congress as manipulative, crooked and indecisive, more recent representations are much harsher, depicting congressional leaders as incompetent, inept and even stupid. Much of this can be attributed to Americans' loss of respect for political institutions in general and Congress in particular. Also, over the course of the 20th century as the presidency has ascended, the role of Congress has diminished. And the prestige of the Congress in the media has dwindled as a result.

The recent Republican ascendancy in the House and Senate, however, has boosted congressional leaders back into the political spotlight and generated plentiful new material for political cartoonists. If history is any guide, members of Congress who become the object of cartoonists' attention may not like what they see.

Joan L. Conners is a Ph.D. candidate in the School of Journalism and Mass Communication at the University of Minnesota.

Not a Pretty Picture 115

"Congressional Pugilists" The Bettmman Archive
1798

"Bosses of the Senate" Puck
Joseph Keppler, 1889

"Pan-Ic in Session"
Thomas Nast, 1881

Harper's Weekly/Oxford University Press

Not a Pretty Picture 117

"Read 'em? I'm too busy protecting 'em."
Bill Mauldin, 1946

"The Accuser"
Rollin Kirby, 1920

Jim Berryman, 1948 — The Washington Evening Star

"Haunted House"
Herbert Block, 1970

"The Butler Did It"
Herbert Block, 1983

Kevin Kallaugher, 1992 — The Baltimore Sun

Reporters rush to the telegraph office with their stories, 1868.

17

Unexpected Consequences—
New Media and Congress

Thomas C. Leonard

The rhetoric was as expansive as all America. Congress would put up the money for "the great highway of thought," building a dream of "making in fact one neighborhood of the whole country." It sounds like breathless talk about the Internet, but actually it comes from the story of the telegraph, which was unveiled 150 years ago in one of the repeated "communications revolutions" that has washed over the Congress. It is a story worth repeating because it sheds light on a recurring question of contemporary importance: when Congress cheers on a communications revolution, what does it get for its money and its high hopes?

Speaker Newt Gingrich knew what he wanted in 1995 when he put Congress on the World Wide Web. "Thomas" (for Thomas Jefferson) is the Web page that gives instant access to the bills and debates in the House. According to the Library of Congress, which runs the service, Thomas is being used more than a million times every month. All of this is part of the Speaker's plan to change "the entire flow of information and the entire quality of knowledge in the country." Thomas, he said, would take power from Washington lobbyists and give it to ordinary citizens "because everybody's an insider as long as you're willing to access it."

Call up Thomas and your screen fills with a bust of Jefferson, head tilted in his best questioning spirit. Perhaps this is because, even in Jefferson's lifetime, a communications revolution had proven to have mixed results for the accountability of Congress, the empowerment of citizens and the legitimacy of government. Before legislators celebrate the communications revolution at the end of the 20th century, they might consider the cautionary tale of earlier breakthroughs.

The Constitution was drafted in secret because the founders did not think they could do their best work with the whole country watching them. The first Congresses attempted to maintain these agreeable working conditions. The Senate was often closed to both press and public in the 1790s, and the House discouraged reporters until the end of that decade. Journalists complained that they could get only the "skeleton of debate." Legislators saw this as political cover, for their arguments could be easily revised before they were cast into print for citizens to see.

Innovations in communication made Congress more accountable in the years between the presidencies of Jefferson and Jackson. The first link between the floor of Congress and the voters at home was the U.S. mail, the key bureaucratic triumph of the young republic. In the early 19th century, foreigners marveled over the growth of the Yankee postal service, just as they were later to note the American mania for telephones, television and computers.

Party newspapers were the new media of this democracy, and they organized political life more systematically than the press of the 18th century. The founders had considered parties to be inherently corrupt and certainly did not design the postal system to nurture them. But exactly that happened as both the legislative and executive branches learned how to subsidize partisan networks of friendly publishers. Editors filled their papers with speeches from Capitol Hill and made the new skill of shorthand the mark of a political reporter.

From the start, there were worries about an information overload and hidden costs in the communication system. Congressmen paid nothing to mail their speeches and so were able to send wagon loads of their addresses into the heartland. Ordinary citizens, however, paid high postal rates for letters. In effect, they subsidized their legislators' franking privilege. And the free distribution of congressional missives provided free copy for partisan newspapers. Political papers filled the village post office "in multitudes like the plague of frogs," according to one discouraged woman.

This first communications revolution for Congress was two things at once—a broadcasting of information across the land and a narrowcasting to constituents in the lawmaker's home district. (Such narrowcasting gave birth to the word "bunk" when a representative speaking on the floor of Congress asked his colleagues not to listen to him because he was only "speaking for Buncombe," that is, to create a record to send to his district in Buncombe County, N.C.)

Stronger terms were used, though, as the mails spread far and wide congressional rhetoric on the divisive issue of slavery. Thomas Jefferson was not sure that the nation could withstand this public debate and called it "a fire bell in the night." Shortly after Jefferson wrote these words, Denmark Vesey led a slave revolt in South Carolina. The authorities found reports of congressional speeches on slavery in his possession. To see that this would not happen again, Congress killed further debates with "gag orders," President Jackson tried to rid the mails of "incendiary material," and white Southerners built bonfires for some of the Northern papers that jammed their post offices. Plainly, communication by itself did not foster harmony or understanding. Antagonists over slavery, knowing more about their differences, girded for battle.

Reporting from Congress was putting politicians on the record, making all regional and partisan differences clearer. In our own time, Speaker Gingrich believes that the legislative process will seem more legitimate as everyone learns where legislators stand. But the history of the early republic demonstrates that political rage can stem from this knowledge. The most brutal assault by one member of Congress on another, the canning of Sen. Charles Sumner by Rep. Preston Brooks in 1856, took place after the hotheaded Southerner had read the full text of a Sumner speech.

The telegraph carried on the communications revolution that opened Congress to the people. The inventor, Samuel F. B. Morse, had won an appropriation of $30,000 on his promise to conquer time and space. When congressmen gathered in 1844 for a demonstration of the device, they were not sure that the money was well spent. "That's what I call pretty thin," one lawmaker said after seeing the bewildering line of dashes and dots. There was no Newt Gingrich of the telegraph, even after the system won praise on Capitol Hill. The wires carried vital political news, such as election results. But lawmakers realized that the telegraph could not meet their primary need to narrowcast their message. The service was much too expensive for congressmen to use for reaching the voters in their districts.

The telegraph, however, was the perfect device for news agencies, which wished to broadcast their words fell into the hands of wire services, whose bold new art was to compress information and to prune rhetoric. Mailbags had nurtured congressional eloquence, but the telegraphy system, which charged by the word, was a ruthless editor of what lawmakers had to say.

Congressional debate was again reduced to a skeleton, this time not by congressmen wary of publicity but by a new breed of reporters at the Associated Press. In the first decades of the telegraph, few newspapers could afford to take more than the two columns of top stories and business. News was what the paying public wanted, not the fine arguments that lawmakers spun. Until well after the Civil War, political detail, analysis and color still came through the mail. The telegraph was the province of stripped-down news reports.

Eventually efficiencies of scale took hold, allowing longer stories to go out quickly by wire (a dispatch sent from Capitol Hill to New York cost one-twenty-fourth as much in 1886 as it had a quarter century earlier). Legislators were pleased to see more of their activities covered as breaking news all across the land. The telegraph helped lawmakers to see beyond the old sectional interests and strengthened American nationalism. Anthropologists know that national feeling depends on the imagination; the wiring of America gave people vivid demonstrations—in news reporting that sparked their minds—that they held something in common.

But anyone who thinks that Congress was better respected once it headed down the telegraphic information highway ought to consult *The Gilded Age* (1873) by Mark Twain and Charles Dudley Warner or "The Treason of the Senate" (*Cosmopolitan,* 1906) by David Graham Phillips. Lobbyists began to dominate Washington in these decades, in part because lawmakers needed more help to navigate through the flood of information that came with an advanced technology. The corruption of lobbying, reported in a timely fashion over the telegraph, made hating the Congress a national pastime.

Congress, where minds were focused on home districts, was not very good at influencing the transnational wire services. The White House, with its national perspective, attracted the people who knew best how to use the new media. Lincoln, for example, had cultivated AP correspondents and used them to manage the news. Such techniques enabled Lincoln to weather the periods when his war policies faltered. And he was only the first of a string of Republican presidents to lean on the wire services by controlling access to information. The AP was called the "Hayesociated Press," because it smoothed the way for Rutherford B. Hayes to become president.

Congress, on the other hand, was slow to exploit the telegraph, just as it would be slower than presidents to use radio and television. New technology may improve the legislative process, but in the United States the chief executive has been the biggest winner with new media.

As Speaker Gingrich tries to change this, he must face the larger lesson of communications revolutions: the beneficiaries are unanticipated. Lobbyists today may find the same windfall enjoyed by political parties and wire services in the 19th century. The experience in 1995 with Thomas is instructive. This database, so useful for tracking bills and issues—and votes—makes it easier for pressure groups to go after lawmakers. Thinking narrowly makes Thomas easier to use, and the service is friendly to single-issue politics. Thomas encourages a certain kind of accountability but makes it no easier to find eloquence, inspiration or the genius of compromise in debate.

Will Congress win our hearts as it gives us more records we can search? Not necessarily. Throughout history, advances in reporting have turned our political order sour at least as often as they have brought sweetness and light. Worse for Speaker Gingrich, Congress has rarely been happy when it has touched off communications revolutions.

Thomas C. Leonard is professor and associate dean of the Graduate School of Journalism at the University of California, Berkeley, and author of The Power of the Press: The Birth of American Political Reporting and News for All: America's Coming-of-Age with the Press.

18

Race, Rules and Reporting

Donald A. Ritchie

"Race in the Newsroom," the *New Republic*'s cover story for Oct. 2, 1995, triggered angry protests from the *Washington Post* because of its exposé of staff resentment against the paper's policies to promote racial diversity. White reporters claimed that while they had advanced by individual merit, the *Post* had bent the rules to hire and promote racial minorities. "We used to say, 'Let's go out and get the best guy in the world,'" asserted one veteran white journalist. 'Let's get the best without regard to anything else.'" But historical evidence suggests the opposite. The *Post* and the rest of the mainstream press in Washington long operated under rules that effectively barred minority journalists. Integration of the Washington press corps was a slow and painful process, complicated by white reporters' intolerance and indifference, discord within the African American press, and rancor between men and women journalists of both races.

Integration of the Washington press corps began with the fight for accreditation. A press pass for either the Capitol or the White House has been the traditional prerequisite for covering national events at the capital. Accreditation was more than a matter of status; it gave reporters admission to the press galleries in Congress and to press conferences throughout the government, provided privileged seating at committee hearings and put their names on the distribution list for countless press releases. Back in the 19th century, when the House and Senate first set up press galleries, the speaker of the House, the vice president and the Senate Rules Committee determined whom to admit. As politicians aiming to please, they tended to admit anyone who applied. Vice President Millard Fillmore granted a woman reporter access to the Senate press gallery as early as 1850. In the 1870s the prominent African American editor Frederick Douglass sat in the Senate and House press galleries. But the galleries also attracted lobbyists who masqueraded as journalists and reporters who augmented their salaries as lobbyists. A series of public scandals caused the Washington press corps to reform itself. Leaders of the pack approached the speaker of the House in 1879 to propose that reporters elect their own Standing Committee of Correspondents. The committee would set rules for accreditation and judge applications.

The first Standing Committee of Correspondents required that reporters file dispatches by telegraph to a daily newspaper, derive the largest share of their income from newspaper work and neither engage in lobbying nor be employed by any government agency. These rules not only eliminated lobbyists but also all women and minority journalists—for reasons completely unrelated to lobbying. None of the 20 women who had sat in the galleries in 1880 qualified for accreditation. At that time, women journalists could get assignments only to cover social news or to write character sketches. They mailed their stories to their papers, since only fast-breaking political news justified the telegraph tolls. Similarly, since the mainstream press never hired black reporters, and since the black press consisted entirely of weekly papers, black reporters could not meet the requirements for accreditation. In later years, women reporters were readmitted gradually, but no black reporter sat in a congressional press gallery again until 1947.

African American journalists' inability to win accreditation was not from lack of trying, especially during the turbulent New Deal years of the 1930s, which stimulated intense demand for news from the capital. Trying to cover the New Deal, black reporters complained that they had "as little chance of interviewing a cabinet officer as of getting an interview with God." Their best news pipeline came through the "Black Cabinet," consisting of such officials as Mary McLeod Bethune, William Hastie and Robert Weaver. Messengers and mimeograph operators also slipped black reporters copies of documents and reported overheard conversations. A few white officials passed information anonymously. Often, however, black reporters could learn what was going on only by reading the *New York Times*.

Even without accreditation, posting a correspondent in Washington lay far beyond the financial resource of most black newspapers. Seeking to fill the void, the Chicago-based Associated Negro Press (ANP) opened a one-man Washington bureau in 1939. Directed by Claude Barnett, the ANP provided weekly mimeographed news stories to its 112-member papers and encouraged reciprocal news sharing among them. Yet black publishers tended to resist sharing news with their rivals. The larger weeklies put out numerous regional editions. *The Pittsburgh Courier,* for instance, published 17 editions from the Pacific Coast to the deep South, and in cities from New York to Detroit. Multiple editions pitted black papers from distant cities against each other for readers and advertising revenue. Partly for that reason, the *Chicago Defender* refused to subscribe to the ANP. Indeed, the *Defender* accused ANP of rewriting its stories for distribution to its competitors. There was truth in the charge: the financially strapped ANP was often little more than a "clipping service," for the same financial reasons that the *Defender* sometimes rewrote its own news from the *Chicago Tribune.*

When the ANP's first Washington correspondent, Alvin White, applied for admittance to the congressional press galleries and presidential press conferences, he found the doors firmly shut. The standing committees insisted that he did not comply with their rules. Steve Early, press secretary to President Franklin D. Roosevelt, advised that a black journalist could meet the rules by filing as a reporter for the *Atlanta Daily World,* which since 1932 had been the nation's first and only black daily. But the *Atlanta Daily World,* with 55 widely scattered weekly papers, was part of the Scott News Syndicate. And it was unwilling to share its unique advantage with papers outside of its syndicate. When first lady Eleanor Roosevelt urged that black journalists be admitted to the president's press conferences, Early explained that the editor of the only black daily newspaper "has never appointed a Washington correspondent, although he has been advised of his right to do so."

The Second World War saw renewed efforts to get Washington news "from a Negro viewpoint." In 1942, competition for the ANP emerged in the newly created National Negro Publishers Association (NNPA). The driving force behind the NNPA, *Chicago Defender* publisher John Sengstacke, hired a correspondent to cover Washington for both the Defender and the NNPA. Rivalry between the two black news organizations took place against the backdrop of a wartime investigation of the black press. The FBI monitored editorials that demanded racial integration of the armed services, which some government officials interpreted as provoking racial unrest. Receiving indications that the federal government might prosecute black editors for sedition, Sengstacke rushed to Washington to meet with Attorney General Francis Biddle. Sengstacke offered to tone down the rhetoric of the black press in return for greater access to official news. "Nobody will talk to us. So what do you expect us to publish?" Sengstacke argued.

Like most government officials, Attorney General Biddle had never given any thought to the absence of black reporters from his press conferences. He agreed to contact other cabinet members and also to urge the president to open his own press conferences to black reporters. At Biddle's request, Steve Early met with Sengstacke and worked out an arrangement that recognized that the NNPA provided news to the *Atlanta Daily World,* even if that paper refused to claim the NNPA's correspondent, Harry McAlpin, as its own reporter. This sufficiently stretched the rules to enable McAlpin to attend the president's press conference in February 1944. "I'm glad to see you, McAlpin," said Roosevelt as he shook his hand, "and very happy to have you here." Despite victory at the White House, the Standing Committee of Correspondents on Capitol Hill rejected McAlpin for membership in the press galleries on the grounds that he did most of his reporting for weekly papers. By opening the door for him, they argued, reporters for other weekly publications would flood the galleries. Since few weekly papers could afford resident correspondents in Washington, McAlpin declared that they had rejected him for his race "rather than by the flimsy technicality publicly stated."

Having sought accreditation by "playing by the rules," the ANP watched the rival NNPA succeed by going over the heads of the White House Correspondents Association. Claude Barnett advised his new Washington correspondent Ernest Johnson not to "shed briny tears" over their failure to win accreditation first. "We will get in," he pledged. Johnson, however, soon found it "physically impossible" to cover all of Washington by himself without access to the press galleries and press offices for news releases and regular sources of interviews. Since the *Atlanta Daily World* also refused to acknowledge Johnson as its correspondent, the ANP claimed that his stories appeared in the new *Dayton Daily Bulletin.* When the Standing Committee questioned the size of that paper's circulation, a frustrated Johnson advised Barnett, "Quote them 10,000 if necessary and let them jump in the river."

In 1946, Republicans won majorities in both the Senate and House, removing Southern Democrats from the chairmanships of the key congressional committees. The first order of business when the 80th Congress convened in January was a debate over the seating of the outrageously racist Sen. Theodore G. Bilbo of Mississippi. The debate held enormous interest for black newspapers, but the NNPA's new Washington correspondent, Louis Lautier, had to stand on line with the rest of the public for a seat in the public galleries. Lautier took his case to Illinois Republican Sen. C. Wayland "Curly" Brooks, who chaired the Senate Rules Committee and who sought endorsement from the *Chicago Defender* for his upcoming re-election bid.

The Standing Committee of Correspondents had rejected Lautier's application by a vote of 5 to 1. The sole vote in Lautier's favor came from committee chairman Griffing Bancroft, a reporter for the *Chicago Sun-Times*. Bancroft voted for Lautier because "it was important that a black man be admitted" and felt that his colleagues based their opposition "more or less on a technicality" whether Lautier was the bona fide correspondent of the *Atlanta Daily World*. Then Sen. Brooks intervened. "I am saying to you gentlemen," he told the Standing Committee, "that you can very easily answer this question by admitting one man." Under his prodding, the Senate Rules Committee voted unanimously to admit Lautier to the Senate Press Gallery. The Rules Committee's jurisdiction did not extend to the House, but the Standing Committee of Correspondents capitulated and voted to admit Lautier to both House and Senate galleries. This brought a blast from the *New York Times'* Kentucky-born Washington bureau chief Arthur Krock, who in his column accused the Senate of forcing the Standing Committee to violate its rules "only because the reporter affected by them is a Negro." Conversely, other African American reporters protested that Sen. Brooks had missed the point if he thought that admitting Lautier alone would solve the "Negro press problem."

No sooner had the Standing Committee accredited the NNPA's Lautier than it received an application from Alice Dunnigan as the ANP's Washington correspondent. Previously a stringer for the ANP, Dunnigan inherited the post by default: Ernest Johnson had resigned, and no male reporter would take the job at the starvation wages that were all that the

ANP could afford. Unaware of the long struggle to integrate the press galleries, Dunnigan simply went to the Capitol and attempted to enter the press gallery. When the Capitol Police turned her away, she protested: "I'm a newspaper reporter, and I'm going wherever those newsmen are going." She applied for formal accreditation and assumed that Lautier gained admittance ahead of her only because he was a man. Then Dunnigan discovered that the ANP had never bothered to endorse her application. "For years we have been trying to get a man accredited to the Capitol Galleries and have not succeeded," Claude Barnett told her. "What makes you think that you—a woman—can accomplish this feat?" To Barnett's astonishment, the Standing Committee accredited Dunnigan in July 1947. She took her congressional press pass to the White House and State Department, making her the first black reporter to hold all three coveted press passes.

Lautier and Dunnigan broke racial barriers in Washington the same year that Jackie Robinson first played for the Brooklyn Dodgers, but the press integrated more slowly than did baseball. Relying on the ANP and NNPA services, few black papers could afford their own exclusive Washington correspondents. The mainstream press remained glaringly white. In the early 1950s the *Washington Post* hired Simeon Booker as its first black reporter. But unable to flag down taxicabs in the District, harassed by police whenever he entered white neighborhoods and uncomfortable eating in the *Post*'s own cafeteria, Booker resigned within a year to return to the more hospitable environment of the black press. Not until years after the civil rights movement had begun, at a time when urban riots broke out during the 1960s, did white newspapers and magazines recognize the need to hire black reporters.

In 1954 the National Press Club voted to admit Louis Lautier as a member. This marked the only time in the club's history that it inducted anyone by a vote of the entire membership. The Press Club was a private organization that rented office space to reporters and provided them a place to meet for drinks after hours, talk over the day's news and play some poker. Although willing to admit a black man, the Press Club continued to bar all women reporters, white or black. Women journalists had formed their own Women's National Press Club, which itself had no black members. In 1947 reporter May Craig had invited Alice Dunnigan to a dinner party of club members, but Dunnigan felt intimidated by the quick-talking women journalists and sat quietly throughout the dinner. She was not invited back until after Lautier had joined the National Press Club. Recognizing the contradiction in their own efforts to integrate the Press Club, women reporters unanimously voted to admit Dunnigan in 1955. She later cited her membership as "one of the greatest things that has ever happened to me during my newspaper career," because it "opened avenues for many exclusive stories and personal interviews with prominent dignitaries." But she resented the long years of working "in the shadow of rejection" by fellow journalists: "seven years of waiting for professional liberals to decide whether they could, in good faith, accept just one minority member into their sacred society."

Women journalists conducted an intense campaign to open the National Press Club. If nothing else, they wanted access to the luncheons where newsmakers regularly spoke. They made a point of asking visiting dignitaries to boycott the National Press Club unless women were able to attend the lunches. Among the few to support them was Soviet Premier Nikita Khrushchev. The club permitted the "ladies" of the press to sit in the balcony for his speech but advised them to leave within a half hour after Khrushchev concluded his remarks.

During the March on Washington in 1963, women journalists also pressed A. Philip Randolph and Martin Luther King Jr. to support their protest against the National Press Club. Ironically, the civil rights leaders declined, explaining their need to reach the mainstream press. Thus they addressed a press club segregated by gender rather than by race, with the men on the floor and the women in the balconies. Art Buchwald grasped the humor in this situation, citing complaints of National Press Club members that "our women were very happy to sit in the balcony until outside agitators from the North came down here and started trouble." Professing to be worried, Buchwald wrote that if the men let the women reporters eat with them, "pretty soon they'll want to dance with us and neck with us, and before you know it all the barriers will be down and they'll be wanting to play poker with us." The National Press Club finally accepted women members in 1971.

As the mainstream press began to cover the civil rights movement more thoroughly, it undercut the black papers by hiring away the best reporters and competing for readers. For survival, the black press shifted its focus from national to local news, causing the ANP to lose business steadily until it closed in 1964. Claude Barnett offered the ANP to the

NNPA, but the publishers rejected his proposal. Soon after, the NNPA's own Washington service also quietly expired, its role being assumed by a United Press International news service aimed at black papers.

For years, African American members of Congress have commented that they observe more black faces on the floor of the House than in the press gallery. The American Society of Newspaper Editors recently reported that only 10 percent of all American journalists are African, Asian, Hispanic or Native American. Although a marked increase over previous findings, that figure remains well below the one-quarter of the U.S. population that those groups collectively comprise. The largest increase in minority hiring has occurred in the broadcast media, which employs twice as many minority journalists as do newspapers and periodicals, hence the affirmative action programs to increase minority hiring at the *Washington Post* and other newspapers that have stirred such anxiety among whites and raised the specter of racial backlash in the newsroom. Although replete with irony, the historical record makes clear that ostensibly race-neutral rules in fact fostered segregation and discrimination. History offers no solace for those who assume that the playing field was ever level.

Donald A. Ritchie is associate historian in the U.S. Senate Historical Office and author of Press Gallery: Congress and the Washington Correspondents.

19

Rayburn, the Workhorse

Joe S. Foote

Sam Rayburn ruled the House of Representatives for two decades with masterful skill and enormous power. He played a decisive role in the passage of the legislation that defined the New Deal. Yet, this legendary speaker did so with hardly any concern about the news media and its impact. Today, it is difficult to imagine how a political leader could refuse to court the national media, stifle their access to public meetings, routinely deny their interview requests and still be regarded as one of the most powerful men of his day. Yet all of these were characteristics of Rayburn's relationship with the press.

Speaker Rayburn and Speaker Newt Gingrich will both be remembered as powerful men of the House, but the difference between their strategies for dealing with the press reveals much about the growing importance of the media in congressional politics. Before taking for granted the solid connection between media success and legislative success, we should look back a generation to Rayburn's speakership, when the connection between politics and media had yet to be made in the House of Representatives. In retrospect, Rayburn's methods for dealing with the press provide a benchmark for measuring the evolution of congressional influence upon the media and media influence on Congress.

Rayburn was speaker of the House from 1940 to 1947, 1949 to 1953 and 1955 to 1961. Having served in the House since 1913, most of Rayburn's adult life was spent in the cloistered halls of Capitol Hill. Through his 48 years there, Rayburn mastered every rule and procedure and knew every member. He was a creature of the House who consolidated power and wielded influence beyond what most speakers could ever imagine.

Being speaker has traditionally been an inside job, but particularly so during Rayburn's day. What counted was protecting the House as an institution, moving legislation from committees to the floor, rounding up votes, assembling coalitions, arbitrating feuds among members, serving as a liaison with the administration and presiding over the House. Far down the list, if considered at all, would be an external role for the speaker as spokesperson for the House or the Democratic Party. Even during the Eisenhower administration when he was the highest-ranking Democrat in Congress, Speaker Rayburn showed little inclination to assume the role of national spokesperson or to speak to the nation through the press. Instead, the speaker prized contacts with reporters mainly because of their value within the House.

Ironically, while Rayburn was wielding great power in the House without reaching out to the nation through the press, presidents were rapidly expanding their own use of the media. From Franklin Roosevelt's administration on, presidents developed numerous outlets for public persuasion. As presidents gained access to a grand national forum, there was no comparable voice of opposition from the Congress. In some cases, the media took on the opposition role themselves, with the three commercial television networks serving as a de facto "loyal opposition" to the president. There is no evidence, however, that Rayburn was concerned about the imbalance between his media exposure and the president's.

To understand how and why Speaker Rayburn could remain so aloof from the important mass media trends swirling around him, one must consider the environment in which the speaker operated. Rayburn's first and foremost love was the House of Representatives as an institution. His instincts and his actions reinforced that link. Bipartisanship had real meaning during his tenure; there was comity between party leaders and they worked together closely, especially in foreign affairs, which was conducted devoid of party divisions during most of the Cold War. Party loyalty, while waning, was still strong enough to respond to a speaker's persuasive call. Most members of Congress were from "safe" one-party districts who could stay in the House as long as they wanted. The seniority system was at its height, giving speakers a small number of important players with whom to deal.

These realities not only contributed to the power of a speaker, but reinforced the insularity of the House of Representatives. It was only natural that the House membership would choose a leader who reflected the insular norms of the institution. Because speakers are chosen by the insiders of the majority party, a speaker's loyalty extends first and foremost to that constituency. In Rayburn's time, a speaker's loyal lieutenant might spend 15 to 20 years on the leadership ladder to work into a position of responsibility. During these apprenticeships, the House's internal reward system reflected Rayburn's maxim "To get along, go along." Rayburn's successor, John McCormack, who was 70 years old when he became speaker, waited through 34 years of congressional service and 20 years as Rayburn's deputy to get his hands on the speaker's gavel. (McCormack had actually first run for speaker in 1934.)

In Rayburn's world, a distant posture toward the press was part of proper behavior for a House leader. House members generally wanted leadership that was fair, impartial and sensitive to their needs. House procedures were organized so that media attention was focused on committee chairs, whose job was to move bills through the legislative labyrinth. The speaker, in contrast, was a facilitator who worked quietly behind the scenes to help the committees realize their goals. If a speaker during this era had taken center stage in the media, there would have been repercussions among the venerable committee chairs.

House members during Rayburn's days never demanded that their leader project his presence beyond Congress. They saw little benefit and great risk in dealing with reporters. Most senior members had achieved their stature and leadership positions without having to depend on the national press. Many members of Congress told horror stories about embarrassment at the hands of aggressive journalists. Speaker Rayburn and his colleagues sought to defend themselves from the media, not to cultivate it.

A telling example of Speaker Rayburn's suspicion of the media and his failure to see opportunity through national exposure came in a letter he wrote in 1957 to Lawrence Spivak, the producer and moderator of NBC's "Meet the Press":

> I do appreciate your wanting me to be on "Meet the Press," but I never go on programs such as yours because some 20 or more years ago I did go on a panel program on the radio and all the folks on the panel got in such an argument that I had enough. The trouble about my going on one program is then I would have no

excuse to say to others that I could not go on their program. It is a chore that I have never relished and one that I doubt if I would be very good. So, at the present I will have to tell you what I tell all of the others, and that is that I do not go on these programs.

Rayburn wrote that letter on the cusp of significant changes in the media's relationship to politics. Broadcast commercials had been a rapidly emerging influence in the 1956 presidential elections. The national press corps was growing in numbers and influence. News conferences were becoming more frequent. Aspiring national candidates like John Kennedy were using their Senate positions as springboards for publicity. The Sunday talk shows and other programs were gaining stature and having to fend off senators and executive branch officials. Yet Speaker Rayburn, indifferent to or unaware of this dynamism, comfortably relied on media experiences from the 1930s to gauge his television-age decisions.

Not only did Rayburn personally choose to avoid the media, but he attached a stigma to others who did not follow him. His frequently used dichotomy between "showhorses" and "workhorses" was not an idle one. A workhorse was a member whose attention was unswervingly focused on the business of the House and was willing to subordinate their own ambitions for the good of the institution. A showhorse was seen as a member impatient with the arcane and laborious workings of the House who would frequently go outside the institution to gain publicity for legislative initiatives. Under Rayburn, as under his predecessors, House members who developed a high media profile were ostracized. Rayburn once said, "When a man has to run for re-election every two years, the temptation to make headlines is strong enough without giving him a chance to become an actor on television."

The showhorse and workhorse categories were mutually exclusive; it was impossible for Speaker Rayburn to imagine how anyone with national prominence gained through the media could be a credible and effective legislator. Only in the "Other Body," the Senate, would a member dare to combine the two. House members had long believed that senators—each of whom sits on more legislative committees than a representative—did not have a legislative mastery equal to that of a representative. And in a representative's mind, a House colleague who courted the media was no better than a know-nothing senator.

Rayburn's antipathy towards media exposure created great difficulties with the television networks during the 1950s, when ABC, CBS and NBC were rapidly encroaching on the power base of the print press and throwing their newly found weight around all over Washington. As television emerged, there was a natural bid for access to the House chamber, committees and capital grounds. In virtually every case, Speaker Rayburn barred the door.

On the opening day of the 80th Congress, Speaker Joseph Martin, who had just taken the chair from Speaker Rayburn after the Republicans captured the House in the 1946 elections, allowed television to cover the swearing-in ceremony. It was a television first and almost a last. The Democrats returned to power in the House and from 1949 to 1953 and 1955 to 1961, Rayburn would once again be speaker. Largely because of his dictates, it was 32 years later before the House floor would be opened to cameras again. The television networks, used to getting access wherever they wanted it, became increasingly frustrated with Speaker Rayburn's inhospitable treatment. They clashed with a speaker whose singular commitment was to protect the members of the House from embarrassment and to preserve the decorum and traditions of the House. Access to the television networks figured far below those priorities. Requests from the media were a nuisance with no intrinsic value.

One of Speaker Rayburn's most controversial rulings was his 1952 decision to ban radio and television broadcasts of House committee hearings. He reasoned that because the House did not allow broadcasts, the ban should extend to committees as well. The speaker said he was "not going to let this thing deteriorate into a sideshow, however good the performance" and firmly believed that he was not trampling on the rights of the broadcast media.

Because Senate committees were accessible to cameras, the ban further isolated the already-uncovered House and enraged some committee chairs who saw the ruling as a one-person edict. The chair of the House Committee on Un-American Activities challenged the ban on cameras in committees in 1957 by allowing a field hearing in San Francisco to be televised. Speaker Rayburn immediately summoned the recalcitrant chair to his office, and no other chair ever tried to circumvent Rayburn's ruling.

Although Speaker Rayburn maintained a low media profile for himself and expected as much from his colleagues, he developed closer relationships with a small group of "insider" reporters than might ever be possible today. To the handful of Rayburn confidantes who faithfully covered the House over the long haul, access to the speaker was unprecedented. His inner circle was even invited to participate in the "Board of Education"—the speaker's end-of-the-day reflection and drinking sessions held in his Capitol hideaway. During these off-the-record sessions, reporters plugged themselves in to the most intimate insider details of the House and its members. In Rayburn's mind, these trusted reporters were different from the rest of the national press; they understood and respected the work of the House of Representatives. They also understood the importance of long-standing personal relationships as Rayburn did and would not sacrifice those relationships for a single story. It was a true symbiotic relationship.

Speaker Rayburn's close friendships with veteran House reporters fit with his broader philosophy toward relationships that formed the cornerstone of his success. As biographer Anthony Champagne wrote, the foundation of Rayburn's power was "his ability to use information networks to build personal loyalties." Reporters were a valuable part of the Rayburn information network; they knew the House and its members well and helped the speaker keep his hand on the pulse of his colleagues.

The glowing aftermath of the "Board of Education" meetings was the speaker's daily five-minute news conference in his ceremonial office just before the House's noon session, where he would outline the day's agenda and answer a few questions. Most of the faces around the speaker's desk were the same old friends he entertained regularly downstairs. It was customary for the senior wire-service reporter, nearly always a Rayburn intimate, to start the questioning.

It was purely an insider's game; questions focused on arcane procedure or mundane scheduling of business. Today's reporters would hardly call it a press conference. Observers not initiated to the process would have a difficult time understanding what was going on. House jargon and parliamentary shorthand punctuated answers. It was the odd day that a reporter asked a penetrating question that did not deal specifically with that day's work in the House.

If a question emerged that the speaker did not like, an aide would call "Time, Mr. Speaker," and Rayburn would quickly make his way to the House floor. Rayburn intimates in the press corps were also careful to warn the speaker when a new face was in the crowd and would frequently tell the newcomer that the speaker's press conferences were off the record. Such protection, provided by gallery "regulars," meant that

Speaker Rayburn was rarely burned by questions during daily press briefings.

While the press conferences were highly constrained and lacking in news value by today's standards, they provided daily access to the speaker of the House of Representatives. On good days and bad, the speaker had to endure at least a few minutes with the press corps. If nothing else, the ritualistic conferences served as a daily reminder of the presence of the media and their importance as a conduit to the public.

For the most part, however, Rayburn so stigmatized the media that his two chief lieutenants and successors, John McCormack and Carl Albert, also felt highly uncomfortable with personal exposure in the press. This legacy was particularly unfortunate because it encouraged McCormack and Albert to negate their role as national spokespersons during the 1960s and 1970s, when presidents made particularly great media strides.

It was not until the mid-1970s, when the impeachment inquiry against Richard Nixon propelled a nameless and faceless House Judiciary Committee into the spotlight, that House members began to see the potential of national visibility. Without such favorable publicity for the House during this climactic event, it is unlikely that its membership would have opened their doors to television five years later.

After 16 years of television exposure, the exclusive distinction between showhorses and workhorses has disappeared; almost every member, backbencher and leader alike, must have a few showhorse characteristics to be an effective workhorse. And now that Speaker Gingrich has propelled himself to leadership through a C-SPAN strategy of national exposure, being a showhorse may be a prerequisite for leadership in the information age.

Little remains of the structure and tone of relations between the speaker and the media that distinguished Rayburn's days in power. It wasn't until Newt Gingrich became speaker that the office assumed a distinctly external quality. From the beginning, Gingrich saw media as a strategic tool for legislative and political success. Unlike Speaker Rayburn, who had the luxury of ignoring the national media, Speaker Gingrich must satisfy demanding internal and external constituencies simultaneously. By giving the media unprecedented access to the congressional leadership, by launching a sharp-edged, high-profile attack on the opposition and by using the full force of the media to relay his

"Contract with America" to voters, Gingrich thrust the House speakership temporarily onto a level of visibility equal to the president's and greatly accelerated a 40-year process of increased public visibility for House speakers.

It was also through high visibility leadership that Speaker Gingrich became a remarkably controversial and polarizing political figure, one viewed negatively by the majority of Americans. While Rayburn never reaped the benefits of media visibility, neither did he suffer the downside risk of becoming a lightning rod for public criticism. Speaker Rayburn's unambiguous internal role undergirded a remarkably stable House that promoted collegiality, fairness and bipartisan cooperation. It remains to be seen whether a universally known speaker who is portrayed as divisive can preserve the kind of collegial environment required for governance.

Today's speaker must be both a highly visible dynamo of partisan activism and a trusted mediator and confidante for all members of the House. Even with the growing importance of media activity to the speaker's new role, there are limits as to how far a speaker can go with his public persona without diminishing his effectiveness in the House. The modern speaker must be nimble enough to bounce back and forth between both roles, realizing that too partisan a profile can diminish leadership effectiveness and trust within the institution while too low a profile defaults an opportunity to influence public opinion. There must be respect for both an "inside" strategy like Rayburn's and an "outside" strategy like Gingrich's. The two approaches are highly interrelated, and finding the optimum balance could prove illusory.

Joe S. Foote is dean of the College of Mass Communication and Media Arts at Southern Illinois University, Carbondale. He was press secretary to Speaker Carl Albert and is author of Television Access and Political Power: The Networks, the Presidency, and the "Loyal Opposition."

Part V

Books

20

Many Questions, Few Answers

Jeffrey R. Biggs

Live from Capitol Hill!: Studies of Congress and the Media
Stephen Hess. Washington: The Brookings Institution, 1991.

Press Gallery: Congress and the Washington Correspondents
Donald A. Ritchie. Cambridge: Harvard University Press, 1991.

Making Laws & Making News:
Media Strategies in the U.S. House of Representatives
Timothy E. Cook. Washington: The Brookings Institution, 1989.

Congress, the Press, and the Public
Thomas E. Mann and Norman J. Ornstein, eds. Washington:
American Enterprise Institute and the Brookings Institution, 1994.

Remaking Congress: Change and Stability in the 1990s
James A. Thurber and Roger H. Davidson, eds.
Washington: Congressional Quarterly, Inc., 1995.

To Renew America
Newt Gingrich. New York: HarperCollins, 1995.

Words are the coin of the realm in this place. Millions of words have echoed through this chamber and found their way to the printed page. Give to the word merchants who labor here continuing sensitivity to the influence of the...word. Help them to appreciate the power of words...to honor, to disparage...to strengthen, to weaken...to build, to destroy....

A decade ago, this invocation by Senate Chaplain Richard C. Halverson expressed concern over the relationship between the Congress and the press. Today this invocation might be interpreted as a request for divine intervention to lift the siege of public scorn that both Congress and the press appear to have jointly imposed on themselves. By its very design, Congress—with its slow, conflictual, diffuse, open and self-critical nature—was fated to be the least popular branch of government. Yet today's stereotyped critique of Congress suggests that the first branch is filled with unethical professional politicians who are out of touch with ordinary Americans, driven to satisfy the legislative needs of special interests who fund their re-election campaigns, consumed with retaining unwarranted perquisites of office and whose political bickering has left the body unresponsive to pressing national needs.

The stereotypical critique of the Fourth Estate is similarly harsh, arguing that the once trustworthy media have fallen prey to the leadership of celebrity national television journalists who have more in common with their political sources than with their audience. The media, in this view, have chosen to pander to the public's baser interest in scandal at the expense of informed opinion and have allowed the dictates of audience share and the economic bottom line to blur any meaningful distinction between news and entertainment. The press has permitted its preference for conflict to contribute to the transformation of a healthy public skepticism into a corrosive cynicism toward public institutions. The media have contributed to the phenomenon that the public no longer differentiates between perception and reality.

As the books discussed in this essay suggest, distinguishing between allegation and guilt, between mere assertion and proven fact, have not, gratefully, lost their relevance to scholarship. And while there was a time when the relationship between Congress and the press was neglected, that time has passed. In preparing a bibliographic essay on trends in political communications, Stephen Hess notes that one scholar read more than 600 works published during the 1980s alone. Taken together, the six books highlighted in this essay cover the 200-plus-year history of the symbiotic relationship between Congress and the press. The authors provide insights for readers to better understand the current low state of public esteem for both institutions, the elements by which the relationship has been characterized historically, and some prescriptions that might contribute to restoring the press and Congress to a better state of health.

"Washington, a city of frequent comings and goings, and many short leases," wrote George Will in *The Leveling Wind: Politics, the Culture, and Other News,* "is so busy trying to divine the future it has little energy left over for learning about its past. A pity, that." "Inside the beltway" has become a popular metaphor for the parochialism, political intensity and self-absorbed concerns of the nation's capital, as opposed to the rest of the country where "real Americans" live. Yet, popular distrust of Washington, as well as between Congress and the press, has roots nearly two centuries old. On Sept. 26, 1789, the day after the House of Representatives approved the First Amendment's protections of a free press, those same representatives debated barring reporters from the House floor. Then, as today, members of Congress wanted to inform the public about legislative activity through the press but recognized that controlling the substance of the reporting was beyond their ability. Historian Donald A. Ritchie notes that in the 1830s one member of the House doubted that the sun had risen a single day that session without some newspaper attack on the legislative branch by the "base, corrupt and penniless scoundrels who beset your Capitol in hungry swarms." By the turn of the century, muckraking journalism's criticism of Congress prompted a similar response as one senator lamented: "The eagerness with which so many people seem to believe ill of public men, the general suspicion of everybody's character and motives, comes pretty near taking away all inspiration for public service."

In a time when many believe that the relationship between the media and Congress is uniquely poisonous, the historic sweep of Ritchie's *Press Gallery: Congress and the Washington Correspondents* is almost singular in assisting the reader to differentiate between the past and present. As an associate historian in the Senate Historical Office, among a handful of congressional staff hired to preserve the institutional memory of Congress rather than to support an individual member's longevity, Ritchie has selected representative correspondents from different eras to demonstrate journalism's transition from a craft to a profession. The journalists portrayed are not all household names, but their careers are characterized in a way that strikes a recognizable chord in our current experience. Horace Greeley, presidential candidate, editor and correspondent of the *New York Tribune,* was "resolute, brilliant, capable, irresponsible, intolerant [and] not above setting things on fire for the fun of seeing them burn." Jane Grey Swisshelm was hired by Greeley in the 1850s to become the first woman admitted to the Senate Press Gallery and was the first asked to leave for breaching the taboo of writing about the private life of a senator, Daniel Webster. Horace White, correspondent and editor of the *Chicago Tribune,* started his personal fortune by speculating in Civil War liquor stocks after learning that Congress would raise whiskey taxes in 1863. White asserted that he secured the tip as a journalist rather than through his patronage job with Congress.

As Ritchie shows, the relationship between newspapers and legislators in the 19th century was anything but professionally distant. Readers expected partisan reporting, and Washington newspapers remained creatures of political parties where a "paper-thin line separated press reporting from promotion." *The National Intelligencer* once agreed to a one-month delay so Daniel Webster could edit what became one of the most widely read speeches in congressional history—his celebrated 1830 attack on the right of states to nullify federal law. This was the era of political oratory, not market research, and words counted. Long-remembered congressional debates focused on the clash of opposing ideas, and it was the printed word that reached the public. Webster, who spoke from notes, would grope for the right word, trying out one synonym after another until he got the right effect. One listener recalled Webster saying: "Why is it, Mr. Chairman, that there has gathered, congregated, this great number of inhabitants, dwellers, here; that these roads, avenues, routes of travel, highways, converge, meet, come together, here? Is it not because we have a sufficient, ample, safe, secure, convenient, commodious port, harbor, haven?" Webster then removed all but the best words before his speech appeared officially in print.

For over a century Congress, not the presidency, was the center of national political news reported from the capital by a relatively small group of journalistic "insiders" whose understanding of legislative policy depended upon a close personal relationship of trust with an equally small group of congressional "insiders." The long-established value of having close ties with sources was fortified by the introduction of bylines and syndicated columns. These innovations raised the identification of Washington correspondents to a national level and gave rise to the familiar lure of being not just an observer but a player.

The dominance of congressional news seemed to end in the 20th century as the clashing voices of Congress ceased to compete effectively with the president's singular voice. Where the president was relatively remote and mysterious, Congress was overly familiar. Where the president's aims appeared coherent, the policies of Congress seemed confused until cemented in a legislative product. And, as the congressional dominance of national news coverage eroded, members of Congress grew to appreciate local and regional coverage as more useful to their re-elections.

Two authors, Stephen Hess and Timothy E. Cook, stand out among many in documenting this new era of the persistent, but largely unsuccessful, congressional efforts to compete with the White House domination of the national press corps. They carefully document the relatively recent emergence of congressional press secretaries and media strategies, while recognizing that when something in Congress gets done, it gets done without a high level of interplay with the national media. By their dissection of how Congress and the press interact, both Hess and Cook persuasively destroy a number of publicly accepted media shibboleths, such as the portrayal of Capitol Hill as an island disconnected from the rest of the country. If representatives have to overcome the danger of becoming detached from constituents, journalists have even fewer direct connections with their readers or viewers.

Hess' Brookings Institution Newswork series began in 1981 with *The Washington Reporters,* which surveyed the personnel and organization of the capital's press corps. It was followed by *The Government/Press Connection,* which focused on how the White House, State Department and Pentagon conducted their press operations, and *The Ultimate Insiders,* with its assessment of why the national media selected some senators as news sources and not others. The latest in the series, *Live from Capitol Hill!,* brings an enormous amount of data (35 separate tables) to Hess' examination of the domination of regional reporting, due in part to the extremely limited access of rank-and-file members of Congress to the national media—particularly television. Hess is not really bothered by the current anxieties over Congress and the press; he simply argues that the system works. The networks may have little time for rank-and-file House and Senate members, but nevertheless those low-visibility members dominate local broadcasts on political news from Washington. In the national arena, Congress fails to read its own polling data, which indicates that despite the generally wasted efforts of press secretaries in nearly every member's office, it is only a handful of senators or representatives who ever attract national media attention. The seeming pervasiveness of television in American life of the '80s and '90s, Hess suggests, has done much to make a few journalists into celebrities. It has done little, however, to make a household name of virtually any member of Congress, despite that institution's elaborate efforts to facilitate coverage.

While Hess offers the congressional organizational blueprint for dealing with the press, Timothy E. Cook's *Making Laws & Making News* chronicles the post-Watergate strategic congressional game plans that emerged following the congressional reforms of the 1970s. These changes introduced gavel-to-gavel television coverage, enlarged subcommittee chair positions for younger members (which undercut the seniority of full chairmen) and encouraged a degree of rank-and-file media entrepreneurship new to the House. Cook lucidly describes these newly independent members of Congress as self-starters with their own power bases and media strategies. They were almost arrogant when it came to accepting any direction from congressional leadership.

The historically high re-election rates that lasted into the early '90s suggest that, at the local level, the Congress-press relationship worked for these new incumbents. At the level of national policy, however, Cook views the media's congressional coverage as being "akin to recirculating air in a building with no windows." Reliance on the "usual authoritative sources" too frequently appears to exclude fresh ideas from less senior members. However, what the public sees and what the Congress does are frequently different. Despite slight national media attention individually, the new members of the 103rd (1992–94) and 104th (1994–96) Congresses, due to their large numbers, internal discipline and their own reform agendas, exerted considerable legislative influence in areas such as crime, the environment, deficit reduction and lobbying reform.

Washington news gathering, as an historic throwback to the 19th century, remains essentially "an interaction among elites" with "one elite reporting to another elite," as Cook puts it. Among the dynamics that have changed, however, are that three or four decades ago, serious members of Congress limited their press exposure. To be a "workhorse" rather than a "showhorse," in Speaker Sam Rayburn's terms, meant to work behind the scenes. Neither the leadership nor rank-and-file member spent time devising a media strategy for advancing legislative goals. The Vandenbergs and Tafts of that era placed less value on stroking reporters, holding press conferences, or getting out a "daily message" as an intrinsic part of the job. Legislative strength came from operating within the Congress. Reporters spent 20 or 30 years covering Congress and developed an intimacy with key members that is probably unknown today.

The very willingness of the press to negotiate a relationship favorable to politicians continues to encourage House members to use publicity and to craft media strategies in pursuit of legislative goals. However, the Cook and Hess books both predate the advent of serious media "Congress bashing," which has undercut the national Congress-press working relationship, and the 1994 congressional elections, where the "Contract with America" seems to suggest for the moment that a national-issue agenda carries more weight with the voters and the national press than a focus on local politics. Until that theory works a second time, however, Hess' and Cook's analyses still have the ring of gospel.

Two books that take account of recent developments in the workings of Congress and the media originate in multidisciplinary conferences convened to assess congressional operations and seek reforms that will counter the public's prevailing cynicism: Thomas Mann and Norman Ornstein's *Congress, the Press, and the Public;* and James Thurber and Roger Davidson's *Remaking Congress: Change and Stability* in the 1990s. Together they offer assessments of today's congressional performance, press converage and the public's disenchantment. These authors suggest that "the nature, volume, tone and content of the coverage" have all become more critical in recent years. Ornstein, Mann and their contributors would suggest that, even in the context of the turn-of-the-century journalistic vitriol, there is a qualitative change in criticism of Congress that goes beyond our having become more thin-skinned.

Congress, the Press, and the Public offers additional data demonstrating that "what you see depends on where you sit": the further the distance from Congress, the more hostile the attitude. Those with the power to set the national news agenda—executive producers and managing editors—are more hostile toward Congress, more content with the current pattern of news coverage and readier to accept the media's departure from traditional professional norms (such as refusing to air rumors without solid, independent, confirmation; distinguishing between the private behavior of public officials and their performance of public duties as subjects for news coverage; and emphasizing coverage of substantive performance over scandal). The new view of Congress also involves journalism's having moved from simply narrating political drama to arbitrating it. Representatives and their staffs make up a steadily diminishing proportion of the sources quoted in news stories about Congress.

In *Remaking Congress,* Ornstein and Schenkenberg's "Congress Bashing" and Roger Davidson's "Wielding the New Broom" offer an important post-1994 update of the themes in *Congress, the Press, and the Public.* If the 1994 elections achieved nothing else, they should have reminded the public that Congress remains subject to the rule of the ballot. The media's widely ballyhooed public disenchantment with "the isolated, entrenched, privileged bastion" in Congress (73 percent disapproval) radically altered the partisan balance of power. Despite a favorable blip for the first 100 days of the Republican Congress, however, polling suggests the public's cynicism toward Congress is not abating. Moreover, public hostility toward Congress has not focused on internal reform as a solution. These essays suggest that the public's continuing anger about politics and government gives every evidence of being "disconnected from concrete information about what is really going on." Why? Because "negativism trumps ideology or analysis every time as a dominant media theme" as Davidson puts it, and citizens are thus more angry than informed.

In the frequently competing agendas of Congress making laws and the press making news, the media has more recently taken the upper hand. Between 1986 and 1992, the Times Mirror Center for the People & the Press measured public attentiveness to major news stories and discovered that of the 294 stories that attracted the most public attention over the six-year period, only 21 dealt with Congress. Of those, the House "bank" scandal story ranked highest, 62nd place, despite an outside counsel's failure to discover any illegality or any loss of taxpayer funds. The story ranked higher than congressional action on the 1986 major revision of the U.S. tax code, the Clean Water Act, the Iran-Contra scandal or the savings and loan banking crisis, all of which arguably had a greater impact on the average American. Journalistically, these more substantive issues were probably more difficult to report on than "bounced checks." The House "bank" scandal was an example of a significant increase in congressional investigations, media revelations and judicial proceedings that have become weapons of partisan institutional combat over the past decade, as Benjamin Ginsberg and Martin Shefter observe (*Politics by Other Means: The Declining Importance of Elections in America,* 1990). Congressional Ethics Committee or special counsel investigations into the behavior of Sen. Bob Packwood, R-Ore., the "Keating Five," or the House "bank" scandals have become more attractive targets for the current media definition of news—news is drama, drama is entertaining and thrives on conflict, and entertainment is marketable. This has become such accepted American wisdom that it is featured in the Sunday comics. As the cartoon character Calvin says to Hobbes, "Finding consensus and common ground is dull! Nobody wants to watch a civilized discussion that acknowledges ambiguity and complexity. We want to see fireworks...."

The more critical tone and focus of the media have not been alone in spawning the historically low public esteem for Congress. Other factors include the complexity of issues such as health care, the public's anxiety with job security and their children's futures, interest groups that focus on creating a sense of anger and outrage in their fund-raising appeals, the general distrust of authority and Congress itself. In a fundamental, partisan sense, Newt Gingrich, the current speaker, and the Conservative Opportunity Society (COS), served as handmaidens to much of the "Congress-bashing" over the last decade. Attacking the institution of Congress represented a successful effort to so undermine its validity, to so repulse the public, that voters would throw the longtime Democratic majority out and allow the Republicans to govern. The 1994 congressional elections ushered in that new Republican majority, the first in 40 years, but it has inherited a Congress that has lost much legitimacy. Even after securing a Republican majority and the speakership, Mr. Gingrich did not moderate his rhetoric in *To Renew America.*

To Renew America is a compilation of old charges. The speaker does not provide new personal or political insights into congressional governance. Indeed, the book's content is drawn largely from the 1993 televised "Renewing American Civilization" lectures that Gingrich has delivered from Reinhardt College in Waleska, Ga. But from the historical perspective, no recent speaker has so enlarged the range of his formal congressional powers or been accorded comparable rapt media attention. Speaker Gingrich has combined a Machiavellian skill at researching and converting voter preferences, prejudices and fears into a legislative agenda with a self-righteous certainty of "vision." Unfortunately, *To Renew America* gives the reader little new beyond that certainty of vision. Nevertheless, given Gingrich's adept use of polling data and the media, it is not surprising that his "Contract with America" has mesmerized the public and, at least temporarily, transferred press attention to Congress.

Consider Speaker Gingrich's "Design Group" of eight lawmakers, handpicked to draft sensitive Medicare legislation outside normal committee channels, and their "CommStat" (communications strategy) press secretaries who have the responsibility for selling the party Medicare reform plan, which they call "the product" and handle as an "account." As *Washington Post* reporters Michael Weisskopf and David Maraniss noted, pollsters were hired to test, much as they did in formulating the "Contract with America," the words used with 400 adults age 50 and older. Topping the list were improve and protect at a 20 percent favorability index each, and preserve at 15 percent. But the word improve was also found to raise expectations beyond what the Republicans intended to deliver. So, "rising in the House just before the Oct. 19, 1995 vote, Gingrich repeated the mantra a final time: 'We want a solution that preserves and protects Medicare for seniors and that sets the stage for the baby boomers.'"

The increasing reliance on polls by Congress and the press to establish a baseline of public concerns is one thing; to use that same polling to replace the traditional legislative debate over alternatives, public hearings on the trade-offs or costs involved and the congressional search for consensus is something else. As Dan Balz and Charles Babcock of the *Washington Post* have suggested, developing a legislative agenda based on "65 percent issues" of public support takes us to a new level of pandering. It transforms the legislative branch of government into a Wal-Mart with responsibililty simply to stock everything the public wants to buy, a Ross Perot electronic town meeting where you register your preference and Congress rubber-stamps the decision with no questions asked.

Are Congress and the media simply caught in a series of combative encounters that must inexorably repeat themselves without abatement? Does serving as the nation's "watchdog" mean that the press treatment of Congress begins with an automatic presumption of malfeasance? Does the political campaign style of congressional coverage end with the election, or does the national media's preference for news about conflict over compromise promote a nonstop process that marginalizes the coverage of governance? Scholarship has yet to offer definitive answers to such questions, but it has provided some perspective to clarify where our concerns should really lie.

"Do the owners and officers of the new CBS see news as a trust...or only as a business venture?" CBS news anchor Dan Rather asked on the March 10, 1987, *New York Times* op-ed page. He was underscoring the industrywide significance of the profit motive in the new structure of American media. As long as a marketplace bottom line dictates their behavior, the press and the public are effectively beyond any outside-imposed reforms other than exhortation. Congress, then, has inevitably emerged as the major target for addressing the inadequacies of the Congress-press relationship.

As the authors of these books remind us, in recent years both Congress and the media have encountered historically low public esteem. But it is the potential long-term undermining of legitimacy that should cause public concern. The authors remind us that some aspects of the Congress-press relationship are constants, and some aspects call for reform. From the beginning, Congress has been destined to rank lower than the other branches of government in public esteem. Congress represents a messy process, but, as when it introduced televised floor proceedings, Congress should be constantly attuned to finding better ways to educate the press and the public about what it does and why. The press has had its high and its low points in a faithful reporting of politics from the nation's capital. As Hess and Cook have argued, for most members of Congress and the majority of press on Capitol Hill, the congressional news that counts is targeted to a local audience and covered by regional reporters. But, as Ornstein and Mann have noted, "national coverage of Congress has been victimized by the blurring of news and entertainment and a pandering to perceived public taste."

The most basic benchmark by which we should measure the job performance of Congress and the press is whether the American people still have faith in the ability of a deliberative representative government to solve problems and of a free press to accurately inform the public. Consider this: a majority of the American public favors conducting national referenda on major issues and requiring the government to give a referendum approved by a majority the same weight as legislation passed by Congress. Of course, if Americans believe that they don't need a Congress, then they may well conclude that they don't need reporters to cover it. Against such unsettling losses of faith, all else pales.

Jeffrey R. Biggs, a former visiting fellow with The Freedom Forum's "Congress and the Media" project, served 21 years in the Foreign Service in positions that included press spokesman and deputy of chief of mission. He served as press secretary/spokesman for former House Majority Leader and Speaker of the House Rep. Thomas S. Foley.

For Further Reading

Baker, Ross K. *House and Senate.* New York: W.W. Norton, 1989.

Bates, Stephen. *The Media and the Congress.* Columbus, Ohio: Publishing Horizons, 1987.

Blanchard, Robert O., ed. *Congress and the News Media.* New York: Hastings House Publishers, 1974.

Callahan, Daniel, William Green, Bruce Jennings and Martin Linsky. *Congress & the Media: The Ethical Connection.* Hastings-on-Hudson, N.Y.: Hastings Center, 1985.

Campbell, Don. *Inside the Beltway: A Guide to Washington Reporting.* Ames, Iowa: Iowa State University Press, 1991.

Cater, Douglass. *The Fourth Branch of Government.* Boston: Houghton Mifflin, 1959.

Clarke, Peter, and Susan H. Evans. *Covering Campaigns: Journalism in Congressional Elections.* Stanford, Calif: Stanford University Press, 1983.

Cook, Timothy E. *Making Laws & Making News: Media Strategies in the U.S. House of Representatives.* Washington: The Brookings Institution, 1989.

Gingrich, Newt. *To Renew America.* New York: HarperCollins, 1995.

Hess, Stephen. *Live from Capitol Hill!: Studies of Congress and the Media.* Washington: The Brookings Institution, 1991.

_____. *The Ultimate Insiders: U.S. Senators in the National Media.* Washington: The Brookings Institution, 1986.

_____. *The Government/Press Connection: Press Officers and Their Offices.* Washington: The Brookings Institution, 1984.

_____. *The Washington Reporters.* Washington: The Brookings Institution, 1981.

Hoff, Paul S. *Beyond the 30-Second Spot: Enhancing the Media's Role in Congressional Campaigns: Congress & the Media.* Washington: Center for Responsive Politics, 1988.

Larson, Stephanie Greco. *Creating Consent of the Governed: A Member of Congress and the Local Media.* Carbondale, Ill.: Southern Illinois University Press, 1992.

Leonard, Thomas C. *The Power of the Press: The Birth of American Political Reporting.* New York: Oxford University Press, 1986.

Mann, Thomas E., and Norman J. Ornstein, eds. *Congress, The Press, and the Public.* Washington: American Enterprise Institute and the Brookings Institution, 1994.

Marbut, F.B. *News From the Capital: The Story of Washington Reporting.* Carbondale, Ill.: Southern Illinois University Press, 1971.

Nimmo, Dan D. *Newsgathering in Washington.* New York: Atherton Press, 1964.

Ritchie, Donald A. *Press Gallery: Congress and the Washington Correspondents.* Cambridge: Harvard University Press, 1991.

Rivers, William L., ed. *The Adversaries: Politics and the Press.* Boston: Beacon Press, 1970.

Rosten, Leo. *The Washington Correspondents.* New York: Harcourt, Brace, 1937.

Sigal, Leon V. *Reporters and Officials: The Organization and Politics of Newsmaking.* Lexington, Mass.: D.C. Heath and Company, 1973.

Summers, Mark Wahlgren. *The Press Gang: Newspapers and Politics, 1865–1878.* Chapel Hill, N.C.: University of North Carolina Press, 1994.

Thurber, James A., and Roger H. Davidson, eds. *Remaking Congress: Change and Stability in the 1990s.* Washington: Congressional Quarterly, Inc., 1995.

Vermeer, Jan Pons, ed. *Campaigns in the News: Mass Media and Congressional Elections.* New York: Greenwood Press, 1987.

Index

Abortion: family leave and, 50
Accountability: of early Congresses, 126; political cover mechanisms and, 10; World Wide Web supporting, 125, 129
Accreditation. *See* Galleries, press; Passes, press
Advise and Consent, 89, 93–94
Affirmative action programs, 131, 138
African Americans, 131–38; alternative news pipelines accessed by, 132–33; civil rights press coverage competition, 137–38; congressional communications empowering, 127; FBI monitoring editorials by, 134; press clubs, membership in, 136–37; press galleries, admission to, 132–36
Afternoon delivery, 64
Albert, Carl, 22, 145
Alda, Alan, 95
Alexander, Lamar, 69
American Political Network, 64
American Society of Newspaper Editors, 138
Anastasia, Albert, 83
Anastasia, Anthony, 83
Animals: in media strategy, 36
Anniversary stories: on signing of Family and Medical Leave Act, 52
Associated Negro Press, 133–36, 137–38
Associated Press: evolution in congressional coverage at, 55–56; executive branch, relationship with, 128–29
Atlanta Daily World, 133, 134, 135

Babcock, Charles, 158
Baker, Ross K., 7–15
Balz, Dan, 158
Bancroft, Griffing, 135
Barnett, Claude, 133, 134–35, 136
Barton, Joe, 67
BBC, 107

Beilenson, Anthony, 60
Berman, Howard, 46
Bethune, Mary McLeod, 132
Biddle, Francis, 134
Biggs, Jeffrey R., 149–60
Bilbo, Theodore G., 135
Bipartisanship: Cold War era, 140
"Black Cabinet," 132
BNA. *See* Bureau of National Affairs
Bond, Christopher, 50
Bono, Sonny, 101
Booker, Simeon, 136
Boxer, Barbara, 68–69
Bradley, Bill: on American values and media, 43; on citizenship and media, 43–44
Britain. *See* Great Britain
Broadcast media. *See* Radio; Television
Brookings Institution Newswork series, 153–54
Brooks, C. Wayland, 135
Brooks, Preston, 127
Browning, Graeme, 65–71
Buchwald, Art, 137
Bureau of National Affairs, 61
Bush, George, 50–51
Business interests: family leave and, 49

Cable Television Consumer Protection and Competition Act, 77–78
California: newspaper coverage of Congress in, 99, 100, 101–2
Camp, Andrea, 51
Capra, Frank, 90–92
Carter, Jimmy, 103
Cartoons, political, 113–23; congressional unity in, 113–14; evolution of congressional caricatures in, 114; examples of, 115–23
CBS: Fulbright Vietnam War hearings and, 86
CCWI. *See* Congressional Caucus for Women's Issues

Celebrities: in media strategy, 36
Champagne, Anthony, 144
Chicago Defender, 133, 135
Citizenry. *See* Public
Citizenship: exercising, 43–44
Civic journalism, 108–9
Civil rights movement: press coverage competition over, 137–38
Clay, William L., 48
Clinton, Bill: Family Medical Leave Act and, 45
Cloture, 60
Clubs, press: minority admission to, 136–37
Cohn, Roy, 84–85
Communication barriers, 7–8; on congressional Web sites, 65–68; declining clarity in political policies as, 108; in first Congresses, 126; House insularity creating, 140–41, 143; journalistic insiderism creating, 14–15, 52; minorities coping with, 132–38; in newspaper coverage, 99–100, 132–33; in slavery debate, 127; technophobia creating, 70; in telegraphy system, 128; in television coverage of floor debates, 75–79
Communications revolutions, 125–29; Congress failing to exploit, 128–29; congressional accountability increased by, 126, 127
Communications strategy. *See* Media strategy
Communications technology: congressional mastery of, 68–69; congressional misuse of, 65–68, 128–29, 142; congressional resistance to, 70, 75–79, 127; distancing congressional-press relations, 29–31, 61–62; speeding up delivery process, 61–62, 63–64; tradition, combined with, 57–58, 60–61, 62
Community, sense of: on Capitol Hill, 63
Compromise: Hollywood representations of, 91, 95; media coverage ignoring, 53–54
Compton, Ann, 29–31
Conflict: left vs. right as dominant model of, 50; media focus on, 53, 156–57
Congress: vs. House of Commons, 105; media strategies aimed at, 23; public perceptions of, 63, 89–97, 150, 155–56, 157, 159–60; regional reporting of, 153–54; relative anonymity of, 99, 154. *See also* House of Representatives; Senate
"Congress Bashing," 156
Congress Daily, 64
Congressional Caucus for Women's Issues, 46, 47
Congressional-constituent relations: communications revolutions and, 125–29; disconnected communications in, 7–8, 65–68, 70; Hollywood as barometer for, 89–97; on Internet, 65–71; legislative complexity hindering, 10–11, 14–15; television coverage enhancing, 77, 79, 82–84
Congressional Directory 1995–1996, 67
Congressional-press relations: agenda item filtering and, 8–9; communications technology distancing, 29–31, 61–62; congressional hearings and, 81–87; distrust in, roots of, 151; House of Representatives neglecting, 22, 140–41, 142, 145; as interaction among elites, 154–55; media focus and, 9, 11–12, 14, 51–54, 156–57; media strategy opportunities in, 39–41; outside media strategy and, 19–25, 145–46; professionalism lacking in, 152, 155–56; recent improvements in, 154; television coverage straining, 75–79, 142–43
Congressional process. *See* Legislative process
Congressional Quarterly, 60, 62, 102
Congressional TV Correspondents Association, 75
Congress, the Press, and the Public (Mann and Ornstein), 155–56
Conners, Joan L., 113–14
Conservative Opportunity Society, 21
Constituencies. *See* Public
Constitution: legislative efficiency and, 9
"Contract with America," 158
Cook, Timothy E., 19–25, 153, 154–55
Corruption: Hollywood representations of, 96
Costello, Frank, 84
Cox, C. Christopher, 66
Craig, May, 136

C-SPAN, 21, 75–79, 106–7; Cable Television Consumer Protection and Competition Act, 77–79; House television cameras experiment, 76–77; network television's response to, 86; potential viewership of, 107; viewer demands for greater coverage by, 76
C-SPAN 2, 78
Cynicism: current public, 87, 150, 155–56, 157; past public, 89–90; rise in, 95–97, 114

Dahl, Robert, 10–11
Daily publications: press gallery membership and, 58–59, 60–61
Daily Telegraph, 106
Danson, Ted, 36
Databases, congressional, 62, 102–3, 125, 129
Davidson, Roger, 155, 156
Dayton Daily Bulletin, 134–35
Democracy: representative vs. direct, 109
Democratic House leadership: contradictory functions of, 23
Dentzer, Susan, 13
Dies, Martin, 82
Direct democracy, 109
Dirksen, Everett, 22
Distinguished Gentleman, 89, 95–97
Dodd, Christopher J., 48–49, 50
Dole, Robert: campaign home page of, 69; family leave and, 50; Gingrich, Newt, on, 21; television coverage of floor debates and, 75, 76
Douglass, Frederick, 132
Dreier, David, 100–101
Dreyfuss, Richard, 48
Drury, Allen, 93
Dunnigan, Alice, 135–37

Early, Steve, 133, 134
Economist, The, 106
Ehlers, Vernon J., 68
Electronic media: bias against, 60; speed of, 61–62. *See also* Internet
Elving, Ronald D., 45–54
E-mail: congressional use of, 66
Endorsements, newspaper, 102
Energy Department: journalists rated by, 107–8
Ervin, Sam, 86

Eshoo, Anna G., 68
Ethnocentrism: in American media coverage, 106, 109–10
Executive branch: current legislative challenges to, 56; greater media attention commanded by, 81, 140, 153; telegraphy system and, 128–29

Family leave, 45–54; business opposition to, 49; disillusionment of press assisting, 51–52; initial media attractiveness of, 46–47, 48–49, 50; measuring effect of, 52; waning media interest in, 50–51
Fax news services, 63–64
FBI: African American press monitored by, 134
Federal News Service, 62
Feedback: congressional Web sites lacking, 65
Fifth Amendment rights: congressional hearings and, 85
Fillmore, Millard, 132
Films, political, 89–97; growing antipathy in, 95–97; media strategy represented in, 91, 92, 95–96; pragmatism prized in, 94–95; progression of congressional imagery in, 89–90, 95, 97; respectfulness in, 93–94; sense of hope in, 91–92
Financial Times, 106
Foley, Thomas, 22–23
Foote, Joe S., 139–46
Ford, Gerald, 103
Fowler, Tillie, 67
Frank, Reuven, 81–87
Friendly, Fred, 86
Fulbright, J. William, 85–86

Galleries, press, 58–59; blurred jurisdictional lines of, 60–61; membership in, 58–59; minority admission to, 131–32, 133, 134–36
Garland, Lillian, 46
Gibson, Tom, 71
Gilded Age, The (Twain and Warner), 128
Gingrich, Newt: on accommodating media expectations, 24, 28; "Congress-bashing" by, 157; on conservative values and media, 28; as cyberspace cheerleader, 65, 71, 125;

on democracy and threat of decay, 27; on exposure, 27; on getting out his message, 27; loyalty to Party objectives rebuilt by, 108; outside media strategy of, 19–25, 145–46; on press coverage since becoming speaker, 27; on religion and reporting, 28; television coverage of floor debates supported by, 21, 76–77; *To Renew America*, 157–58; unconventional route to leadership by, 20–22
Ginsberg, Benjamin, 157
Gorlin, Rachel B., 33–41
Gorney, Cynthia, 46
Government/Press Connection, The (Hess), 153
Gramm, Phil, 69, 106
Granada Television, 109
Great Britain: media coverage in, 105–9
Greeley, Horace, 151–52
Greenhouse, Linda, 48
Guardian, The, 106
Gunderson, Steve, 25

Halleck, Charles, 22
Halley, Rudolph, 83, 84
Halverson, Richard C., 150
Hastie, William, 132
Hayes, Rutherford B., 129
Hearings, congressional, 81–87; declining public interest in, 86–87; Fifth Amendment rights and, 85; Kefauver committee's influence on, 82–84; star-making potential of, 84–85; theatricality of, 81–82
Hess, Stephen, 150, 153–54, 155
Hill, Anita, 87
Hill, The, 63
Hiss, Alger, 82
Hoekstra, Peter, 76
Hollywood. *See* Films, political
Home pages. *See* World Wide Web sites
House Administration Committee: electronic mail study by, 66
House "bank" scandal, 156–57
House of Commons: vs. Congress, 105
House leadership: Democratic vs. Republican, 23–24, 56. *See also* Speaker of the House
House of Representatives: insularity of, 140–41, 143; national visibility potential recognized by, 145–46; Senate, attitudes toward, 142
House Republican Conference: home page for, 68
Hoyer, Steny, 76
HR 770, 50
HR 2020, 47
HR 4300, 48
Hyde, Henry, 50

Identity creation, 33–34, 84–85
Ideology, political: in British vs. American print media, 106; Hollywood decrying extremism in, 94
Information overload: in early postal system, 126
Information resources. *See* Databases, congressional
Inside media strategy, 143–45, 146
Insiderism, congressional, 140–41
Insiderism, journalistic, 13–15, 52, 143–45, 152
Integration, press corps, 131–38
International affairs: American press neglecting, 106
Internet, 65–71; capabilities of, 66; congressional discomfort with, 70; congressional mastery of, 68–69; congressional misuse of, 65–68; as next step in congressional coverage, 64
Internet users: growing number of, 70; as swing voters, 70–71
Iran-Contra hearings, 86
Irresponsibility: in media practices, 107–8, 156–57

Jefferson, Thomas, 125, 127
Johnson, Ernest, 134–35
Johnson, William, 101–2
Jordan, Barbara, 86

Kasich, John, 14
Kaufman, George S., 92
Kefauver, Estes, 82–84
Kennan, George F., 86
Kennedy, Edward M., 48
Kennedy, Patrick, 48
Kerrey, Robert, 67
Khrushchev, Nikita, 137
KidsLink, 68–69
Kimball, Richard, 103

King, Martin Luther, Jr., 137
Kolbe, Jim, 67
Krock, Arthur, 135

Lamb, Brian, 75–79
Lautier, Louis, 135, 136–37
Leahy, Patrick J., 68
Legislative efficiency: Constitution and, 9
Legislative-executive branch relations: greater media focus upon, 56; media coverage competition between, 81, 140, 152–53; new technologies and, 128–29
Legislative process: clearly communicated, examples of, 14–15; complexity of, 9–11, 14; ideal vs. real, 8; media avoidance of, 11–12, 14, 52, 86, 99–100; media understanding of, 13–14; public understanding of, 7, 8, 10–11, 15, 53; subtleties of, 53–54; television's effect upon, 59
Lehrer, Jim, 13–14
Lenhoff, Donna, 47, 51–52
Leonard, Thomas C., 125–29
Leveling Wind, The (Will), 151
Lewin, Tamar, 46
Library of Congress, 125
Lincoln, Abraham: news management techniques of, 128–29
Live from Capitol Hill! (Hess), 153
Lobbying: reporters prohibited from, 132; telegraphy system and, 128
Lowry, Edward G., 11
Lugar, Richard, 69

MacArthur, Charles, 92
"MacNeil/Lehrer NewsHour," 13–14
Magazines. *See* Periodicals
Making Laws & Making News (Cook), 154
Mann, Thomas, 155–56
Maraniss, David, 158
McAlpin, Harry, 134
McCarthy, Joseph, 84–85
McClellan, John, 85
McCormack, John, 22, 141, 145
McQuern, Marcia, 101
Media: British vs. American, 105–10; comprehensiveness of, 106; ethnocentrism in, 106, 109–10; as image creators, 33–34, 84–85; integration of, 131–38; irresponsibility in, 107–8, 156–57; journalistic insiderism of, 13–15, 52, 143–45, 152; left-right analysis dominant in, 50; liberal biases in, Newt Gingrich on, 28; politicians avoiding, 22, 140–42, 145; profit motive in, 159; public perceptions of, 150; skepticism in, 107, 113–14; transition from craft to profession, 151–52. *See also* Congressional-press relations; Electronic media; Newspapers; Radio; Television
Media expectations: politicians meeting, 24–25
Media focus: on behind the scenes analysis, 55; communications technology altering, 29–31, 60, 128; conflict attracting, 53, 156–57; on congressional matters decreasing, explanations for, 99–100; on current legislative-executive branch relations, 56; international affairs, neglecting, 106, 109–10; legislative and executive branches competing for, 81, 140, 152–53; legislative process, neglecting, 11–12, 14, 52, 86, 99–100; public awareness affected by, 52, 100; sense of urgency required to sustain, 51; television's effect upon, 60, 82–83
Media proliferation: agenda item filtering and, 8–9; evolution of, 58–64
Media strategy: Hollywood representations of, 91, 92, 95–96; of past congressional leaders, 22–23, 139, 145, 146; post-Watergate, 145, 154; recent Republican Party, 108. *See also* Inside media strategy; Outside media strategy
Media strategy opportunities, 34–41; celebrities as, 36; congressional hearings as, 82-85; Internet, neglecting, 65–68; Internet, optimizing, 68–69; press relations and, 39–41; quotes as, 37; sound bites as, 34–35; spin control and, 35–36, 49; spontaneity in, 37; substance selling and, 37–39; visual elements as, 35–36; void in newspaper coverage of Congress as, 100–101
Medicare, 158
"Meet the Press," 141–42

Menefee-Libey, David, 100
Merson, Melissa, 57–64
Michel, Robert, 11, 22
Minority hiring, 131, 137–38
Morse, Samuel F. B., 127
Mr. Smith Goes to Washington, 89, 90–92
Multiple referrals, 9

National agenda items: filtering, 8–9
National Federation of Independent Business, 49
National Intelligencer, 152
National Journal, 64
National Negro Publishers Association, 133–36, 138
National Press Club, 136, 137
Network television: congressional resistance to, 142–43; C-SPAN's influence on, 86
New Republic, 131
Newspapers, 99–103; African American, 133–36, 137–38; British vs. American, 106; information sources for, 102–3; large vs. small, coverage provided by, 99, 101–2; politicians editing, 152; positive efforts by, examples of, 101–2; postal system nurturing, 126; press galleries and, 58–59; principal forms of congressional coverage by, 100; superficial congressional coverage by, 99–100
New York Times, 106
NFIB. *See* National Federation of Independent Business
Nielsen Media Research: on Internet users, 70
Nixon, Richard, 82
NNPA. *See* National Negro Publishers Association
North, Oliver, 86

Omnibus legislation, 10
O'Neill, Thomas: Gingrich, Newt, and, 21; live congressional television coverage and, 59; media strategy of, 22
Opinions, political: inconstancy of, 109
O'Reilly & Associates, 70
Organized crime: Kefauver committee and, 82–84
Ornstein, Norman, 155–56
Outside media strategy, 19–25, 145–46; inside strategy, balanced with, 146; political necessity of, 20; precedents of, 22–23; weaknesses of, 24

Palo Alto Weekly, 101–2
Parliament: media coverage of, 105–6
Partisan newspapers, 126, 152
Passes, press: bypassing, 62, 132; minority access to, 131–32, 133, 134–36
Periodicals: press gallery for, 61
Phillips, David Graham, 128
Pittsburgh Courier, The, 133
Policy, political party: declining clarity in, 108
Political cover: of first Congresses, 126; procedural complexity and, 10
PoliticsUSA, 64
Polling: reliance on, 158
Postal system, 126–27
Poynter, Nelson, 102
Preminger, Otto, 93–94
Press Gallery (Ritchie), 151–52
Primaries, 1952 presidential, 84
Print media. *See* Newspapers; Periodicals
Professionalism, journalistic, 152, 155–56
Profit motive, 159
Project Vote Smart, 102–3
Props. *See* Visual elements
Public: congressional hearings, declining interest in, 86–87; Congress perceived by, 63, 89–97, 150, 155–56, 157, 159–60; cynicism of, 87, 89–90, 95–97, 114, 150, 155–56, 157; Family and Medical Leave Act, awareness of, 52; legislative process, understanding of, 7, 8, 10–11, 15, 53; media perceived by, 150. *See also* Congressional-constituent relations

Quotes: as media strategy opportunities, 37

"Race in the Newsroom," 131
Racism: in Washington press corps, 131–38
Radio: congressional resistance to, 143; press galleries and, 58, 59
Radio-Television Correspondents Association, 29
Rains, Claude, 91

Randolph, A. Philip, 137
Rather, Dan, 159
Rayburn, Sam, 22, 139–46; background of, 139–40; House insularity and, 140–41; inside circle of reporters embraced by, 143–45; media strategy strengths of, 146; news media avoided by, 139, 140, 141–42; news media banned by, 143; on "workhorses" vs. "showhorses," 142
Reconciliation bills: understanding of, 13–14
Regional reporting, 153–54
Remaking Congress (Thurber and Davidson), 155, 156–57
Republican House leadership: greater press coverage of, 56; media strategy leading to, 108; unity of, 23–24; World Wide Web usage by, 67–68
Ritchie, Donald A., 131–38, 151–52
Riverside Press-Enterprise, 101
Robb, Charles S., 68
Rockefeller, John D., IV, 67
Rodino, Peter, 86
Roll Call, 62–63, 77
Roosevelt, Eleanor, 133
Roosevelt, Franklin, 134
Rosenstiel, Tom, 89–97
Rothberg, Donald, 55–56
Roukema, Marge, 50
Ruff, Jackie, 51
Rusk, Dean, 85–86

Scandals: excessive media attention to, 156–57
Schroeder, Pat: family leave and, 47–48, 51
Seduction of Joe Tynan, The, 89, 94–95
Senate: House members perceptions of, 142; television changing rules of, 60
Senate Rules Committee, 135
Senator Was Indiscreet, The, 89, 92
Sengstacke, John, 133–34
Sexism: at ANP, 136; in Washington press corps, 132, 136, 137
Shefter, Martin, 157
Shields, Mark, 13–14
Sinclair, Barbara, 23
Skepticism: in congressional coverage, 107, 113–14
Slavery: communication barriers in debate of, 127
Smith, Hedrick, 21

Smith, Lamar S., 67
Social cohesion: achieving, 108–9
Sound bites: as media strategy opportunities, 34–35
Speaker of the House: media strategies of, 22–23, 139, 145, 146; traditional tasks of, 140, 141
Spin control, 35–36, 49
Spivak, Lawrence, 141
Spontaneity: in media strategy, 37
Staffs, press: wider interactivity in, 55
Standing Committee of Correspondents, 132, 134, 135, 136
Stevenson, Adlai, 84
Stevens, Robert T., 85
Stewart, James, 90
Substance: selling, 37–39
Sumner, Charles, 127
Swisshelm, Jane Grey, 152

Talent, James M., 68
Tarplin, Rich, 48–49
Taylor, Paul, 52–53
Technology. *See* Communications technology
Technophobia, 70
Telegraph, 127–29; congressional debate edited by, 128; lack of congressional support for, 127; rhetoric surrounding, 125
Television: British vs. American, 106–7; Cable Television Consumer Protection and Competition Act, 77–79; congressional hearings, relationship with, 81–87; congressional resistance to, 75–79, 142–43; early successes of, 143; government technicians producing, 75, 77; Kefauver committee's influence on, 82–84; live congressional coverage by, 21, 59–60, 75–79, 82–87, 143; press galleries and, 58, 59; Senate rules changed by, 60; as theater, 81
Thomas, Clarence, 87
"Thomas" Web page, 125, 129
Thurber, James, 155
Time constraints: electronic media coping with, 61, 62; media coverage quality affected by, 53–54, 57–58, 61; political cartoons, effect on, 114
Times Mirror Center for the People & the Press, 71, 156
Tobey, Charles, 83

Tocqueville, Alexis de, 15
Tolchin, Martin, 63
To Renew America (Gingrich), 157–58
Town meetings, 109
Tradition: communications technology combined with, 57–58, 60–61, 62
"Treason of the Senate, The," 128
Truman, Harry, 84
Twain, Mark, 128

Ultimate Insiders, The (Hess), 153
Un-American Activities Committee, 82, 143
Unsoeld, Jolene, 36

Vesey, Denmark, 127
Vietnam War: Fulbright's investigation of, 85–86
Visual elements: as media strategy opportunities, 35–36

Waco hearings, 87
Waldholtz, Enid, 63
Walker, Robert S., 70
Warner Brothers Television Network, 78
Warner, Charles Dudley, 128
Washington Alert, 62
Washington Post: race relations at, 131, 136, 138
Washington Reporters, The: (Hess), 153
Watergate era, 86, 145

Weaver, Robert, 132
Webster, Daniel, 152
Weekly Report, 102
Weinberger, Martin, 99–103
Weisskopf, Michael, 158
Welch, Joseph, 85
White, Alvin, 133
White, Horace, 152
White House Correspondents Association, 134
Whitewater hearings, 87
"Wielding the New Broom," 156
Wilde, Oscar, 41
Will, George, 151
Williams, Shirley, 105–10
Wire services: telegraphy system and, 127–29
Women: child-care issues, 45–47; press club membership, 136–37; press gallery admission, 132, 135–36
Women's Legal Defense Fund, 47
Women's National Press Club, 136–37
Wood, Kimba, 45
World Wide Web sites, 65–71; congressional accountability, as source for, 125, 129; congressional mastery of, 68–69; congressional misuse of, 65–68; interactivity as key to, 69–70
Wright, Jim, 22
Wyden, Ron, 66

Zuckman, Jill, 51